Once again Wesley Duewel has captured the preeminence of prayer in a Christian's life. By this skillful presentation of snapshots of fourteen wonderfully used Christian men and women of the last five centuries, he reveals afresh how each one was effectively used by their Savior Jesus Christ. One quickly discerns how prayer is bonded to the Christian's holy life, producing fruitfulness in ministry. Reading the life of the famous missionary Adoniram Judson is worth the complete book!

JOHN E. KYLE
Senior vice president, Evangelical
Fellowship of Mission Agencies

Heroes of the Holy Life is a great service to contemporary Christians, especially to youth. Great biography is available, but not often read in a media-oriented culture. These thorough, yet short, biographies open up a wonderful door to all Christians seeking a deeper walk with Christ. I predict that the next great movement in the church will be a search for the deeper life. This book will whet the thirst of many who long to move beyond entry-level faith to deep and satisfying discipleship. At some point in life most Christians are faced with the words of Jesus, "If anyone would come after me, let him deny himself and take up the cross." It is this decision that precedes the filling of the Holy Spirit that distinguishes the "Heroes of the Holy Life." Modern seekers will find this book an inspiration and a guide.

JAY KESLER
Chancellor, Taylor University

Also by Wesley L. Duewel

Ablaze for God
Mighty Prevailing Prayer
Revival Fire
Touch the World through Prayer

Heroes *of the* Holy Life

Wesley L. Duewel at the grave of John Hyde ("Praying Hyde") in Carthage, Illinois.

Heroes *of the* Holy Life

Biographies of Fully Devoted Followers of Christ

Wesley L. Duewel

ZONDERVAN™

GRAND RAPIDS, MICHIGAN 49530 USA

ZONDERVAN™

Heroes of the Holy Life
Copyright © 2002 by Wesley L. Duewel

Requests for information should be addressed to:
Zondervan, *Grand Rapids, Michigan 49530*

Library of Congress Cataloging-in-Publication Data
Duewel, Wesley L.
  Heroes of the holy life : biographies of fully devoted followers of Christ / Wesley L.
Duewel.
    p. cm.
  Includes bibliographical references (p.) and index.
  ISBN 0-310-24663-6
  1. Christian biography. I. Title.
BR1700.3.D84 2002
270'.092'2 — dc21
[B]   2002008361

Scripture quotations are from the King James Version.

Interior design by Todd Sprague

Printed in the United States of America

02 03 04 05 06 07 08 /❖ DC/ 10 9 8 7 6 5 4 3 2 1

Contents

Foreword

No literature outside of the Bible can bring more inspiration and challenge to Christian devotion than reading the stories of men and women who have walked with God. It makes the transforming truth of Christian doctrine come alive.

That is why this book can be such a blessing. Wesley Duewel opens a window into the lives of some choice saints of old. Although the glimpse is very brief, the reader sees something of the factors that, working together, filled their ministries with grace and glory.

In the unfolding narratives, recurring patterns of lifestyle emerge: a discipline of prevailing prayer, constant recourse to the Word of God, fasting, compassion for people, zeal for evangelism, sacrificial giving, a burden for revival—traits that undergirded and constrained their holiness.

Common to their lives, too, was a deep, abiding sense of the presence of the Lord. Since these saints came from varying cultures and traditions, the details are different in each instance, of course. But the reality of the experience remains the same. These stalwarts of the faith reach a point in their lives when, by complete surrender to Jesus Christ, they move from self-centeredness to self-denial; from weariness and dissatisfaction in labor to radiant joy in service; from inner defeat to overcoming victory and overflowing love in the fullness of the Spirit.

What characterized these heroes of the holy life may seem distant to us today, so accustomed we are to mediocrity in the church. Yet the love and power that they manifested is the privilege of every follower of Christ, whatever may be our appointed task. I can say that reading these accounts of what God has done in other people has made me want to press on to higher ground, and, I trust, this will also be true of you.

ROBERT E. COLEMAN
Distinguished Professor of Evangelism and Discipleship
Gordon-Conwell Theological Seminary

Preface

Told within the following pages are the stories of fourteen men and women, your Christian brothers and sisters, who were tremendously blessed and used by God.

All my life I have been challenged by the biographies of people who were totally committed to Jesus Christ, and I have had a desire to share their stories with others. I pray that these chapters will be a blessing to you and will introduce you to a few of God's wonderful children you will want to seek out and get to know when you get to heaven.

God bless you and make you a blessing to others.

Note: Although I personally use the New International Version of the Bible, that version did not exist when these Christian heroes were alive. The quotations of Scripture attributed to them in this book all come from the King James Version.

WESLEY L. DUEWEL

Francis Asbury —————

Ablaze for God Till Death

Forward for God and Holiness

Francis Asbury (1745–1816) was the circuit rider so ablaze for Christ that one biographer wrote, "He coveted our entire continent with such a passion he appeared anxious to lose his life in the work."[1]

From New England to the Carolinas and from the Atlantic to Kentucky, Francis rode horseback in the pursuit of souls. Some sixty times he crisscrossed the Allegheny Mountains, often at places where roads were nearly nonexistent. Sometimes he rode his horse; sometimes he led the weary animal. In spite of a weak body, frequent illnesses, and, at times, feet swollen with painful rheumatism, he drove himself ever forward. Often his food was game hunted and then cooked on a campfire. He forded streams and was often drenched with rain. His few possessions were in his saddlebags, and when he could find no frontier cabin, he pillowed his head on a saddlebag or stone. He was tormented by ticks and mosquitoes. Unafraid, he braved the dangers of wild beasts, and he faced and escaped stalking Indians.

In Francis's final years he often had to be lifted into his saddle. Even when his friends had to tie him in his saddle, he insisted on traveling to preach wherever there was opportunity. At times he had to be supported by two people in order to deliver his message, and at other times he preached sitting down. He is rightly honored as the father of American Methodism.

Francis had a godly mother who loved to read her Bible and the sermons of John Wesley, founder of Methodism (who was forty-two years older than Asbury), and George Whitefield (Wesley's coworker). Francis began to read by age five or six, and soon he was reading the Bible on his own. He loved to read and reread the account of Moses and other Bible history.

The schoolmaster at the village school was a tyrant and beat Francis day after day with his leather belt until again and again Francis begged not to go to school. "I can't stand to be beaten every day," he said. But there was no other place to get schooling. Francis took off his shirt one day and showed his mother twenty-four deep red bruises across his back. Weeping, his mother said, "Remember that while you are in school I am on my knees praying for you," she said. At thirteen he dropped out of school.

SAVED AND FILLED WITH THE SPIRIT

At the same time, Francis began to seek the Lord in a prayer meeting in his home. He also kept his reading habit, his favorites being the diaries of Wesley and Whitefield. At age fifteen he was converted. He recounted that at sixteen, one day when he was praying in an old barn with a friend, he "experienced a marvelous display of the grace of God, what some might call sanctification, and . . . was indeed very happy."[2] From then on, Francis never turned back. At seventeen he was placed in charge of a Methodist "class" as its spiritual leader. At eighteen he was appointed a "local preacher" of the Methodists. He began traveling to nearby towns and preached three to five times per week.

Following John Wesley's instructions, Francis rose at four o'clock each morning to pray. Then he would head out on his newly purchased horse, Thunder, to visit the poor and the diseased.

He could hardly tear himself away from the homes of the poor. Their sorrows were his sorrows, and his money was their money.

Francis's greatest joy was seeing people commit their lives to Jesus. He loved to see crowded congregations sing the great salvation hymns of Charles Wesley and Isaac Watts with hands raised and eyes filled with tears.

At twenty-two Francis was "fully admitted" to the Methodist Conference by John Wesley, and he began receiving regular ministerial appointments. He wrote, "I will not trade my saddle for a seat in the House of Lords." He attended his first conference in Bristol, where John Wesley preached.

TO AMERICA

When in a sermon Wesley called for volunteers to go to America with the gospel, Francis rose to his feet, tears flooding his eyes.[3] It meant saying farewell to his parents and his girlfriend, never seeing them again. Though often lonely, he lived the rest of his life as a bachelor. John Wesley trusted Francis and appointed him but gave him nothing for his journey. Other friends gave him some clothing and ten pounds. He boarded the ship for the fifty-four-day journey to Philadelphia.

Francis arrived in Philadelphia on October 27, 1771, and went to a service that very night. The next night he preached his first sermon in the New World. The following day he met a woman who had carried her child fourteen miles to attend the service and was now starting home again. Francis was deeply moved. He said, "Maybe the Lord sent her to preach to us! We're going to have to work harder. The New World desperately needs the Gospel."

PLANNING AND PLANTING CHURCHES

Francis stayed ten days in Philadelphia and discovered that Methodists in the United States had not established circuits, though they had planted a number of local churches. It was a two-day trip to New York, so Francis made arrangements to preach along the way. Once in New York, he immediately began preaching in homes and churches. But his heart soon became restless, longing to get out beyond the city and find places to plant congregations of new believers. Every day he planned or preached. He determined to start the same circuit pattern in America that John Wesley had begun in Britain, where there were already forty circuits.

The message Francis preached to the New York believers was "Let us not sleep as others do, but let us watch and be sober." He was troubled that the two leaders of Methodism in the States were content to stay in the city. He felt his call from God was to "spread scriptural holiness to every city and hamlet in America." To initiate the fulfillment of his continent-wide vision, Francis began to make short trips to nearby places and hold services everywhere he could. He dreamed and prayed about establishing circuits all across America and longed for ten preachers to help him. He was soon launching out beyond the cities, blazing new trails, sleeping in frontier cabins, and swimming rivers, always planning how to reach the settlements beyond.

The years that followed were filled with unending ministry. In 1772, within a year of Francis's arrival in America, John Wesley appointed him as his assistant, making him leader of all the Methodist work in the country. He was only twenty-seven. After one year, John Wesley sent out Thomas Rankin and appointed him over Francis. Francis accepted this move with sanctified grace and continued to pour his heart and soul into the work.

This was a difficult period for ministry. By 1776 the United States had declared independence from England and war had broken out. Rankin returned to England, as did many of the other Methodist leaders. John Wesley sent a letter to America urging loyalty to the British crown. This upset many Americans who began to feel that the Methodists were disloyal.

Francis regretted Wesley's letter but loved Wesley as a person. Pressures from those who thought the Methodists were disloyal increased, and Francis had to go into hiding for a time. A letter Francis wrote to friends in Britain expressing his loyalty to the States was intercepted, and when government leaders discovered he was not disloyal, he was once more free to carry on his ministry.

SUPERINTENDENT IN AMERICA

In 1784 John Wesley appointed Francis Asbury and Thomas Coke joint superintendents of the American work. Francis still had one great passion: to see the continent of America evangelized for Christ. Coke, however, organized missionary ventures to different parts of the world. He crossed the Atlantic eighteen times, residing at times in Britain and at times in Ireland. Thus, the burden and responsibility for America was increasingly on Francis's shoulders.

ANTISLAVERY

Francis met a former slave named Harry Hosier, who was wonderfully saved but unable to read or write. God had called this prayer warrior to preach. Francis sometimes invited Hosier to travel with him, and soon Hosier became even more popular a speaker than Asbury. That was no problem for Francis. All he wanted was to see more souls saved.

Francis was grieved with slavery. After lunch with George Washington, he urged him to sign an emancipation document. Washington told him he agreed with him but that he felt this was not the time to sign such a document.

ASBURY'S CARE FOR HIS CIRCUIT RIDERS

The circuit rider's life and ministry was so rugged before 1800 that half of Francis's circuit riders died before age thirty. From 1800 to 1844, half of them lived to be thirty-three years of age. Of the 672 circuit riders of whom we have record, two-thirds were able to continue that ministry for twelve years.[4] They poured out their souls and their health. Francis exhorted his circuit riders, "We must reach every section of America—especially the new frontiers. We must not be afraid of men, devils, wild animals, or disease. Our motto must always be FORWARD!"[5]

Francis had a special burden for his riders. As he multiplied circuits and appointed new circuit riders, he added the name of each one to his daily prayer list, which contained hundreds of names. He encouraged them to live simply and to remain single so they could apply themselves to the gospel ministry without hindrance. They were to preach each day at noon, and their themes were to be free grace, instant salvation, and sanctification through the infilling of the Holy Spirit and holy living. He advised them to keep a disciplined schedule:

1. Rise at four each morning.
2. Spend one hour in prayer each morning from four to five, and one hour from five to six in the evening.
3. Read from six o'clock each morning till noon, with an hour off for breakfast, feeding your mind and soul on the Bible and good books.[6]

THE MORE, THE BETTER

Francis was constantly time conscious. If he could find two places to stop and preach during a day, he was glad. If he could find three or more, so much the better. Regardless of the winter weather, he pushed on. "I must ride or die," he wrote. As much as he was able, he used his riding time praying or reading his Bible, a commentary, or some other spiritual book. He stopped in each settlement and in many homes, preaching wherever he could find listeners. He visited jails to evangelize condemned criminals, and he walked with them to the place of execution.

As John Wesley advised preachers, Francis kept a journal from the beginning of his ministry. One can read such quotes as these:

— "The Lord enabled me to preach with power."[7]
— "I felt divine assistance."[8]
— "There is a considerable work of God."[9]
— "We had a powerful meeting."[10]
— "Thanks be to God, I had power in preaching."[11]
— "Oh, how I wish to spend all my time and talents for Him who spilt His blood for me."
— "I have nothing to seek but the glory of God; and nothing to fear but His displeasure. . . . If I have to beg

from door to door, . . . I will be faithful to God, to the people, and to my own soul."[12]

HOLINESS UNTO THE LORD

Francis believed that the church was to consist of born-again believers separated from the world, who believed in a definite cleansing experience of the Holy Spirit after the new birth, which then was demonstrated by a holy life. Here are more quotes from his journal:

— "It is for holiness that my spirit mourns."

— "Bless the Lord, O ye saints! Holiness is the element of my soul. My earnest prayer is that nothing contrary to holiness may live in me."

— "How I long to be more holy—to live more with God, and for God!"

— "This was a day of much divine power and love in my soul. I was left alone and spent part of every hour in prayer, and Christ was near and very precious."

Francis had three great strategies for evangelism and a holy church. The first was widespread use of circuit riders. The second was the use of quarterly and annual conferences. He attended and presided at as many of these as possible. A typical quarterly conference would start on Saturday and continue through Sunday evening. People slept on floors, benches, the ground, under wagons, or with neighbors. Sunday morning opened with a love feast. This was strictly for the faithful. During the feast, water and bread were passed around and participants drank and ate together. They testified, prayed, quoted Scripture, sang hymns, and shouted the praises of God. The morning service began at eleven o'clock. It began with baptisms followed by a long sermon and the Lord's Supper. The Sunday evening service was evangelistic in nature. It was not uncommon to see hundreds coming forward to pray.

Francis's third strategy for evangelism and a holy church was the camp meeting. The first interdenominational camp meeting was held at Cane Ridge in Kentucky in 1801. Thousands from almost all denominations came from far and near, and the meeting continued night and day. Attendance varied from twelve thousand to twenty-five thousand people. Hundreds fell prostrate under the mighty power of God. At times two, three, four, and even seven preachers addressed different parts of the crowd at the same time. "The heavenly fire spread in almost every direction."[13] A revival movement was sparked among the churches, and in many places the Presbyterians and Methodists united their labors in camp meetings. By 1811, through Francis's encouragement, the Methodists had four hundred camp meetings of their own, and within ten more years there were nearly a thousand. Among those who frequented camp meetings and sang the gospel hymns was Nancy Hanks, the mother of Abraham Lincoln.[14]

By this time Francis Asbury had become the best-known person in America, even preaching to the House of Representatives in Washington.[15] His work was spreading far and wide, but he was getting weaker and weaker in body. Nevertheless, he drove himself on to the very last days of his life. When he could no longer ride horseback, he was carried in a horse-drawn sulky to his next appointment and then was carried into the church or home, where he would sit and preach. He kept winning souls, ordaining preachers, and moving from camp meetings to conferences.

DEATH AND GLORY

A year before Francis died, he wrote, "My eyes fail. . . . It is my fifty-fifth year of ministry and forty-fifth of labor in America. . . . But whether health, life, or death, good is the will of the Lord: I will trust Him; yea, and will praise Him; He is the strength of my heart and my portion forever—Glory! Glory! Glory!"[16] During Francis's last several days, he was still traveling by sulky and speaking. On March 31, 1816, as his speech began to fade, he lifted his hand, and his face radiated a heavenly joy. "His face was the face of an angel."[17] The family he was staying with and other friends gathered around for a service. One of his coworkers asked, "Do you believe that Jesus is precious?" Francis was too weak to answer but raised both of his hands, and in a few moments his head rested on his coworker and he passed away at age seventy-one.

⌐∞

When Asbury arrived in America there were 1,160 Methodists. When he died, there were 214,235. He had ordained more than three thousand ministers and preached more than seventeen thousand sermons. More than fourteen thousand Methodist "classes" had been formed. The Methodist movement had become the fastest-growing denomination in America, including one in every forty people in America.[18]

Asbury was temporarily buried where he died; his remains were later taken to Baltimore. Twenty-five thousand people, out of a total Baltimore population of about fifty thousand, marched in the burial procession in love of Asbury. The National Historical Publications Commission of the United States Government in 1951 chose sixty-six great Americans whose writings were to be preserved for America. Among these are George Washington, John Adams, Thomas Jefferson, Abraham Lincoln, and Francis Asbury.

In 1924 President Calvin Coolidge dedicated a magnificent bronze statue of Asbury mounted on an obviously weary horse. It stands on a fifty-five-ton granite pedestal at an intersection in Washington, D.C.

Arnold J. Toynbee, one of the great historians of the twentieth century, wrote that the "modern English-speaking world was saved in the eighteenth and nineteenth centuries by the Methodists."[19] This is true. One of the greatest and holiest of these was Francis Asbury.

Duncan Campbell

Part 1: Revival in the Hebrides

D uncan Campbell was born February 13, 1898, in a godly
highland Scottish home and grew up to become a minister of the United Free Church of Scotland. His father was
song leader in the local church. His mother led the children in
daily family devotions during the morning, and then, after they
left for school, she sat down by the fireside and prayed for them.

In 1913, while playing the bagpipes at a dance, the Holy Spirit
convicted Duncan by the memory of Christ on the cross. As soon
as he finished the number he was playing, he apologized and left
the dance. As he walked the three miles home, he passed the hall
where each week he attended Sunday school. The lights were on,
so he went inside. His father and two female evangelists—workers in The Faith Mission, an interdenominational home evangelism organization that sent its "Pilgrims" out two by two to
evangelize the British Isles—were holding a night-long prayer session. Duncan went in and sat down beside his father. When his
father stopped praying, there beside him sat the son for whom he
had been praying!

As one of the evangelists read Job 33:14—"For God speaketh
once, yea twice, yet man perceiveth it not"—Duncan was so con-

victed by the Spirit that he held on to the seat to try to stop trembling. He got up and walked out of the service. Twice before he reached home he fell on his knees and asked for God's mercy. When he reached home at about 2:00 A.M., he was amazed to find his mother on her knees praying for him. Duncan went to the barn and began to pray.

In moments Duncan was able to trust God's promise in John 5:24: "Verily, verily, I say unto you, He that heareth my word, and believeth on him that sent me, hath everlasting life, and shall not come into condemnation; but is passed from death unto life." With joy he went back to the kitchen and told his mother. They knelt together beside the fireplace as his mother burst out, "Oh God, You are still the God who answers prayer!"

Duncan continued to attend meetings held by the two Faith Mission evangelists. And on Sunday afternoons he and his mother went from house to house to read the Bible and pray with their neighbors.

In 1917 Duncan was a machine gunner for the British forces in World War I and was in charge of a platoon in the Flanders campaign. Some thirteen thousand British soldiers were killed within a few hours. He prayed, "Oh, God, get me out of here, and I will serve You with my whole heart."

In April 1918 Duncan was in one of the last cavalry charges of the war. His horse was shot from under him, and he lay severely wounded on the ground. He was rejoicing in Jesus but distressed that he still had carnality in his heart. As he lay there, he repeatedly quoted Hebrews 12:14, "Follow . . . holiness, without which no man shall see the Lord." He grieved that he had won so few to the Lord.

Just then another charge was ordered and a Canadian horse group charged over him. A horse's hoof struck him in the spine and he groaned. When the enemy was chased back, the Canadian whose horse had wounded Duncan's back remembered Duncan's groan. He went back and found him bleeding and praying, "Lord, make me as holy as a saved sinner can be" (a prayer he remembered from the writings of Robert Murray McCheyne, revered

Presbyterian leader). Instantly the Holy Spirit swept through his soul, cleansing him. Duncan said, "At that moment I felt as pure as an angel." He knew he had been filled with the Spirit.

In joy Duncan began to quote Psalm 103 in Gaelic (an ancient language understood by many highland Scots and some Irish) as he lay in the casualty clearing station. Within moments seven Canadians who were also lying there were blessedly saved as they heard him pray. The reality of the Spirit's presence flooded Duncan's heart. He eventually recovered.

After the war Duncan began to go house to house to pray with people and lead them to the Lord. In time he realized he needed training. He enrolled in a nine-month training course for evangelists at the Faith Bible College in Edinburgh, Scotland.

Finishing his course, Duncan was immediately zealous for the Lord. In one community the farmers were busy with a late harvest. Duncan canceled the meetings for a week and joined them in harvesting the crop. Then he resumed his evangelism. The meetings were at once filled with the people whose respect he had won. In another area, Duncan held crowded meetings, and God's blessing was beyond anything they had known for twenty-five years.

One day Duncan and an Irish fellow Pilgrim called on a farmer who spoke only Gaelic. This Irishman understood no Gaelic whatever. As they were ready to leave, Duncan called on the farmer to pray. He began at once in Gaelic, and his coworker instantly understood it perfectly. It was Pentecost repeated.

At one place on the island called Skye the Pilgrims' ministry was difficult and was being rejected. One night Duncan prayed all night in a barn while three young ladies prayed until six in the morning at a separate place for God to come in power. The next night God did come on the meeting in power. One woman was so convicted of her sins that she cried out, "I am lost! I am lost!" That night she was saved. Even whole families were won to Christ. And drunkards were saved, delivered, and called to be witnesses for Christ. God worked in homes, on the roads, and in the meetings.

Duncan continued in brief evangelistic campaigns, or "missions," as they were called, until July 1925, when he resigned from

The Faith Mission. He was married about that time, and he began humble ministry with the United Free Church of Scotland. In 1930 he was ordained on the island of Skye.

Duncan went into pastoral ministry for a number of years. He was known for emphasizing his points by a bang of his fist on the pulpit. At times he would dispense with the order of the service and say, "The Holy Spirit has taken charge of this service." The congregation would then go to prayer until the presence of the Lord filled the church. One night God's presence was so real that one of the ladies moved back from where she was sitting because she felt unworthy to sit right beside the Lord, as it seemed to her for the moment that she was doing.

Regularly each morning Duncan spent several hours before breakfast reading, studying, and praying. He would cycle to visit people in his town and in nearby towns. On one occasion people seemed to see the glory of God covering his face. But in time he became discouraged and dissatisfied with his ministry. He returned from a convention and went straight to his study and to his knees. God met him in power, and he felt again the mighty love of God sweeping over him like waves of the sea. God renewed his call to evangelism and gave him a vision of hell with multitudes from Scotland drifting to their doom.

Duncan felt led to reapply to The Faith Mission, although he had been pastoring for twenty-three years, since his marriage. He was now fifty, and the mission was accustomed to using only younger people as Pilgrims. Nevertheless, he began to evangelize on Skye again. One minister said he had not seen such power in meetings in over twenty years. Home meetings were held, and people invited neighbors and friends. Out of respect for the minister, people would stop their work and come to hear him. He held as many as seven home services in a day.

One day as Duncan rode his motorcycle, he experienced a near tragedy as a car, a truck, and his motorcycle almost collided. The car plowed through a hedge into a field. Duncan was thrown off the motorcycle but unhurt. Duncan told no one, but several months later as he was visiting a bedridden woman, she said,

"That's the man I saw in a vision." She told the exact day and hour of the near tragedy and told how she had been gripped by an urgency to pray for him until two o'clock that day, when she received peace. That was the exact time of God's deliverance.

LEWIS AWAKENING

God had sent revival to the island of Lewis and Harris (one island with a double name) in the outer Hebrides off the northwest coast of Scotland repeatedly from the time of the awakening in 1828 until 1939. In 1949 a number of Christians were again praying for God to send revival. One pastor felt that God had given him a promise of revival harvest in his congregation, and his wife had been given a dream in which she saw the church filled with people and a stranger in the pulpit.

In the village of Barvas, Reverend James Murray MacKay and his church leaders prayed for months for revival. Two elderly sisters—Peggy Smith (age eighty-four and blind) and Christine Smith (age eighty-two and almost bent double with arthritis)—prayed for everyone in the village, house by house every night. They were physically unable to attend the services, but they labored on in prayer. On the other side of the village, seven young men prayed three nights each week for months for God to send revival.

One night the Holy Spirit came on the young men as they prevailed on their knees. That very morning he had given Peggy Smith a vision of crowded churches and hundreds of people coming to God. She sent word to Pastor MacKay: "God has promised that He will send revival. You should call the church elders for special prayer." They prayed for several more months.

While Pastor MacKay was attending a convention, he asked the speaker to suggest someone he thought would be able to conduct revival services in his church. The speaker suggested Reverend Duncan Campbell of Edinburgh, who could also speak Gaelic. Pastor MacKay returned to the island and went to see the Smith sisters, and Peggy told him the Lord had told her the name of the preacher who was going to come—his name was Duncan Campbell! The minister contacted The Faith Mission headquarters, and Duncan was able to free his schedule so that he could come within days.

The second night of the meeting the awesome presence of the Holy Spirit came on the people, convicting them of sin. As the service closed, there was a tense silence. The people left the building. A young deacon moved his hand in a circle over his head and whispered, "Mr. Campbell, God is hovering over. He is going to break through. I can hear already the rumbling of heaven's chariot-wheels."

In a moment the church door opened. There stood the entire congregation outside, gripped by the Holy Spirit. They did not want to go home. Other people, drawn by the invisible power of the Spirit, began to gather as they came from their homes. Deep distress over their sins was visible on many faces.

The congregation poured back into the church. The awesome presence of God convicted people of their sins, and they began to groan and cry to God for mercy. Others began to praise God as they received the assurance of salvation. Years of prayers were answered. Strong men cried to God for mercy. The people finally went home praising God for salvation.

But God was not finished yet! About 2:00 A.M. the people came back from their homes, although no further meeting had been announced. Many were saved as they prayed in the street. It was a night of salvation and revival.

That revival night the sisters prayed again for the village, house by house, throughout the night. The next night buses arrived from other parts of the island filled with people who had heard that revival had come. Within days people were being saved in homes, barns, loom sheds (where the famous Harris tweed is woven), and by the peat stacks.

God was answering mighty prevailing prayer in the Hebrides revival. When Duncan first preached in Barvas, God's people agonized in prayer for hours and hours and sometimes all through the nights. Then people gripped by the Spirit of God streamed to the church; and when the church was filled to capacity, great crowds gathered around the church. Scores were brought under conviction, and the revival spread to every part of the island.

And always there was the same amazing work of the Spirit. Young people, who before this time could not be induced to come to church, came in scores and under conviction of sin. They broke down and wept and prayed before God. Drunkards of the deepest dye were also won for God and became bright witnesses for him.

For five weeks in Barvas, Duncan conducted four services nightly: 7:00 and 10:00 P.M. and 12:00 and 3:00 A.M. An expression frequently used in those days was, "The power of God swept through the place," or "The power of God swept over the gathering."

Devout Christians who had been pouring out their hearts daily for unsaved neighbors were suddenly gripped by the realization of their own lack of a pure heart and began pleading with God to give them clean hands and a pure heart (James 4:8). Then God's fire fell, and neighbors began to be convicted of their sin. Duncan believed that "we shall not get revival by filling our churches with men, but by getting the men who already come to our churches filled with God." Revival spread to other parts of the island, and Duncan said the community was "saturated with God."[1]

A man came to a pastor's home asking for prayer. The pastor said he had not seen him in the service. He replied that he had not been in the service but "this revival is in the air. I can't get away from the Holy Spirit."[2]

Another man refused to attend the services at first. Duncan went to his home and prayed for him. That night he felt, "I'm lost, really lost. There is nothing but hell for me." He fell to his knees and prayed a few sentences, asking God for mercy. The joy of sins forgiven flooded his soul, and he leaped up in "an ecstasy of love for Jesus and thought he was going straight to heaven."[3]

A young bus driver was so gripped by God that he stopped the bus and pled with people to repent. He said he was sure someone was hearing God's call to salvation for the last time. Before the return journey, one man who had been on the bus died in tragic circumstances.

A prayer warrior who lived miles distant from Tarbert said he was in his barn praying when suddenly a light flooded around him. It was the exact hour God's Spirit came in power in the meeting and many were saved. Some people were mightily convicted of sins while working in the fields, others while riding their bicycles down the road. People were powerfully converted in many places.

As Duncan began a series of meetings in Arnol, people kept aloof, so the Christians had an evening of prayer in the home of an elder. Near midnight Duncan turned to the local blacksmith and asked him to pray. He rose and began to pray. Suddenly he prayed, "Oh, God, You made a promise to pour water on him that is thirsty and floods upon the dry ground, and, Lord, it's not happening! Lord, I don't know how the others here stand in your presence . . . but, Lord, if I know anything about my own heart, I stand before You as an empty vessel, thirsting for You and a manifestation of Your power." He halted then prayed, "Oh, God, Your honor is at stake, and I challenge You to fulfill your covenant engagement and do what You promised to do!"[4]

"At that moment the house shook. Dishes rattled in the sideboard as wave after wave of Divine power swept through the building!"[5] A minister standing beside Duncan said, "Mr. Campbell, an earth tremor!" Duncan remembered the Scripture, "And when they had prayed, the place was shaken where they were assembled together; and they were all filled with the Holy Ghost" (Acts 4:31). Immediately the community came alive with an awareness of God, and salvation came to many homes on the following nights.

Another time in a revival campaign the atmosphere seemed oppressive, and it was difficult to preach. Duncan asked this same boy to lead in prayer. As he began to pray, he quoted from Revelation 4. He began to sob and called out, "O God, there is power there. Let it loose!" It was as if a hurricane of the Holy Spirit swept into the building. God poured out floods of blessing. Some were weeping, others praying with their arms raised to heaven. God came and took charge. Revival spread.

While revival meetings were being held in one place, a group of fourteen young men were standing outside the parish hall (which was used for dances and for many types of social functions) planning for a dance. While they were standing there, one of the young men said, "I have the feeling that we should increase the order of beer, because for some reason I feel this is going to be the last dance held in this community." The others asked him why. He himself was an unsaved, godless person, but he said that somehow he felt the revival was going to come to their area and that there would never be another dance held there. Suddenly the Holy Spirit came on those young men, and they fell to their knees in the road, crying out to God for mercy, and within an hour all fourteen were converted.

Some years later, Duncan felt led to accept an invitation on Sunday to go to this community. At the close of the service, when he went into the vestry with the minister, several elders of the church were gathered there. The minister told him that every one of these elders, except for one man of eighty-five years of age and the pastor himself, were converts of the revival held many years before. A number of these elders were those young men who were standing beside the parish hall deciding on the beer they should buy for the dance.

Duncan Campbell told me that one night the service was over at about 1:00 A.M. Just then word came that revival had come to another church several miles away, and people had gathered there and were waiting for Duncan to arrive. Some two hundred people along with Duncan started together across the fields to take a shortcut to the crowded church. As they were going along the way, suddenly they heard the sound of heavenly music in the skies. (The same thing had happened during the revival in Wales and also during the revival of Jonathan Edwards, though little is told about it.) When this happened, a number of the unsaved people in the group fell to their knees and began to cry out to God for mercy. These people had a tremendous belief that when Christ comes it will be the final Judgment Day, and they were suddenly afraid that Christ was coming back and they were unprepared. As they knelt there in the glen, thirty-five people were saved.

God seemed to put his seal on the ministry of Duncan in unusual but divine ways. Perhaps the people to whom he ministered lived in an expectation and hope that God would indeed manifest his presence. May God give us a greater hunger for his working, whether seen or unseen.

Duncan Campbell ——————

Part 2: God's Hand in the Scotland Revival

During the revivals in Scotland, two teenage girls, one sixteen and one seventeen years of age, were converted, and God placed on their hearts a prayer burden for their people. Revival had taken place fifty miles from their hometown, but hearing of the revival, they began to pray for their own community and asked another godly young woman there to join them in prayer two nights a week from 10:00 at night until 5:00 in the morning.

After several weeks of these all-night prayer sessions, Duncan Campbell was awakened at 2:00 one morning and felt led to go to the community where these girls were praying. He knew nothing about their prayer. As he was traveling to this town, he saw a young woman along the roadside weeping. He got out of his car, went to her, and asked her if he could be of some assistance to her. It was not uncommon in those days of revival to see people in different places kneeling and repenting of their sins, crying to God for mercy on their souls. Duncan presumed that this woman was under such conviction that she might need some help.

She said to him, "No, you cannot help me. No man can help me."

Duncan got out his Bible, thinking that by reading some Scripture to the young woman he might be of assistance.

Then she looked up at him and quoted from the Song of Songs, "As the apple tree among the trees of the wood, so is my beloved among the sons" (2:3). Weeping, she told him how burdened she was for revival in her parish area and how she had been praying at 2:00 A.M. for such a revival when God showed her that Reverend Duncan Campbell, the man used by God in the other revival, would be coming to her parish area.

Duncan then told her that he was the man she had been praying about.

Immediately the girl threw her arms around Duncan and wept and wept and wept. They went to her parish, and God came on the scene in mighty revival power.

BERNERAY

On Easter Monday in 1952 Duncan was speaking in Hamilton Avenue Presbyterian Church at The Faith Mission convention. At the beginning of a service he heard the name Berneray. Berneray was a small island with a few hundred inhabitants off the coast of Lewis.

Duncan looked around, but no one was speaking to him. He bowed his head and prayed. Again he heard the word distinctly, "Berneray." Still no one was there to speak to him. A third time it was repeated. While the congregation was still singing, Duncan turned to the chairman of the convention sitting beside him and said, "The Lord has told me that I am to leave at once to go to Berneray."

"Why," said the chairman in astonishment, "you can't do that! You are to speak tomorrow morning."

"But what do you do when the Lord says Berneray?" Duncan asked.

"Why, I guess you go to Berneray," the chairman said.

Immediately Duncan picked up his Bible, put it in his attaché case, and walked off the platform. He walked to the hotel, put his things in his suitcase, and called a taxi. Then he went to the airport and asked for a ticket to Berneray. "We have no flight to Berneray," he was told.

Duncan did not go home. Instead, he flew to Harris and asked at the airport how to get to Berneray. He was told to go to the seashore and find a boatman who would be willing to take him. Taking his suitcases to the shore, he asked a man working on a boat what he would charge to transport him to Berneray. The trip would require all the money in Duncan's pocket except for a few pennies. The boatman put Duncan's suitcases in the boat and took him across the water to the shore of Berneray.

Reaching Berneray, the boatman set Duncan's suitcases on the shore and started back to Harris. A steep bank arose in front of Duncan, and he could not see what was on top. He told me later, "Now mind you, I had never met anyone from Berneray or received a letter from Berneray. I had never had a contact with that place." He lugged his suitcases up the bank and saw a young man plowing in a field and trudged over to where he was working.

Duncan asked the man, "Do you have a church on this island?"

"Oh yes," was the reply.

"Please go to the pastor and tell him Duncan Campbell has arrived."

"We don't have any pastor who lives here on the island," the man answered.

"Do you have an elder living here?"

"Oh, yes," he said.

"All right," Duncan said, "go to the nearest elder and tell him Duncan Campbell has arrived."

The man stared at him almost as if he were crazy. Then he started across the field. Duncan was so weary he sat down on his suitcase.

In about half an hour he saw the man walking rapidly toward him. "The elder said to tell you the meeting will be at nine o'clock. He has already sent out invitations. He has your room ready." He picked up Duncan's suitcases, and Duncan followed him.

When they arrived at the elder's home, the elder greeted him warmly.

Duncan asked him, "How did you know I was coming?"

The man had heard how God had used Duncan in the Harris revival, and three days earlier, when Duncan was preaching at Bangor, Northern Ireland, the elder had spent the whole day praying in his barn for God to send revival to Berneray. God gave him a promise—Hosea 14:5: "I will be as the dew unto Israel"—and assured him that Duncan Campbell would be there in three days.

The elder's wife had heard her husband praying in the barn, "Lord, I don't know where he is, but You know. And with You all things are possible. You send him to the island." The elder was so sure God would answer that he sent out announcements.

That night the first service was ordinary. The next night, as Duncan was ready to leave the church, someone came to the door and called for him to come. When he got to the door, he found the congregation so gripped by the Spirit of God they could not leave, and they were standing as a body of people outside the church. The elder said to Brother Campbell excitedly, "He has come. He has come!"

"Everybody come back in," Duncan called in his strong voice.

The people poured back into the church. In a few minutes many were sighing and praying. Sin-burdened souls began to call on God. Many were saved and transformed that night and in the following days. The entire island was shaken.

☙

Duncan was regular and persistent in his private prayer. He sought to begin each day with God. Written on the flyleaf of his own Bible were these words of Lieutenant General Sir William Dobbie: "I have never found anything to compare with the morning-watch as a source of blessing when one meets God before meeting the world. It is a good thing to speak to Him before we speak to other people, to listen to His Word before we listen to the voices of our fellowmen."[1]

In April 1958 Duncan was appointed principal of The Faith Mission Bible College in Edinburgh. Friday forenoons were given to prayer. He gave burning messages to the students. He would say the name Jesus in such a sacred way that the students felt they were standing on holy ground.

On March 4, 1960, God was very present during the students' prayer time. One student said, "It seemed that if I lifted up my head I would look on God." Many wept as wave after wave of the Spirit's power flowed over the students. "Then heavenly music was heard which seemed to fill the room above where they were kneeling; it was incredibly beautiful and harmonious, such as no orchestra could symphonize, and called to mind Zephaniah 3:17, 'He will rest in his love, he will joy over thee with singing.' "[2]

Twice before, during the Lewis revival, Duncan had heard heavenly melodies. Once while he was walking through a glen in the early morning hours the skies seemed to be filled with angels praising. Another minister who was present cried out for joy, "This is heaven! This is heaven!"

The message of holiness and revival burned like a fire within Duncan. At the Lisburn, North Ireland, convention in 1964, he went to his room to pray after breakfast. The chairman was alone in the dining room. Suddenly "the brightness of the presence of the Lord seemed to surround the chairman. He felt so unworthy to be in such a manifestation of God's presence that he went out the door into the flower garden. Everything there seemed to be shining with the same presence of the Lord, and he was melted to tears and went back inside. Just then Duncan, face all aglow, entered. 'God has given me a vision of revival for Ireland,' he said. 'God will visit the island through small bands of praying people in the country districts.' "[3]

All day God's presence lingered near. That evening, after his final message, Duncan pronounced the benediction. The organist attempted to play, but her hands were powerless to touch the keyboard. For over a half hour everyone was so gripped by God's presence that no one moved. Then some began to weep and pray. In the heavenly stillness at least four people heard indescribable sounds from heaven. Only they heard them. After one of the services a farmer said, "You never hear Campbell preach without going home praying."

In a short series of meetings in Aberdare, South Wales, after the second service a prayer meeting continued until 3:00 A.M. Several Christians took off from work to pray the entire next day. That night after Duncan had preached for an hour, six young men sitting together all saw "the glory of God" descend on him. They were gripped with a holy fear and fell on the floor weeping. The fear of the Lord gripped many of the congregation, and people began to repent and restore relationships with one another. One of those present said, "We learned that it is God, not man, we need today."[4]

In 1967, while Duncan ministered in several churches in Canada, God gave him a vision of Canada aflame with revival fire from coast to coast. God showed him it would begin at the Ebenezer Baptist Church in Saskatoon, Saskatchewan. Three years later the Canadian revival broke out in the church where Pastor William L. McLeod had been preparing the church for revival for more than three years. That is where revival came. Revival blessings were poured out. Many came to the Lord, and two thousand revival teams went out to churches across Canada and abroad to testify to God's presence and power. The Canadian Revival Fellowship continues to send out revival teams to churches to this day, and God has given special blessings in many places.

Duncan's body began to weaken in 1971, but he planned a full program for the year. He went to Lausanne, Switzerland, to teach in Youth With A Mission's School of Evangelism in March 1972. His last message was on 1 Corinthians 9:26, "So fight I, not as one that beateth the air." His last words to the students were, "Keep on fighting, but see that you are fighting in the love of Jesus." At 2:00 A.M. he had a heart attack. He lingered for four days and died during a sudden further heart attack on May 28, 1972.

I treasure the times with him in his home and in my home and the times spent arranging a few services for him on his first visit to America. I treasure most sitting by his side as he told me revival stories. What a humble but fearless and anointed man of God he was—a Spirit-filled instrument of God! May God give us more such holy people today.

GIVE US A GREATER HUNGER

Give us a greater hunger, Lord,
Than we have ever known.
Help us to wait in one accord
Until Your power is shown.
Keep us, Your children, on our knees
Beseeching You with mighty pleas
Till floods of blessing like the seas
Sweep over all Your own.

Give us a sense of urgency
That will not be denied.
Give such desire Your work to see
Till ease we cast aside.
Give us soul-hunger and soul-thirst
Till hearts with longing almost burst,
Till we could wish ourselves accursed (Rom. 9:3)
If souls but reach Your side!

Lord, now begin Your mighty work;
Make bare Your holy arm.
O God, forbid that we should shirk
Or to this age conform!
Reveal Your Spirit's mighty power;
Oh, come upon Your Church this hour!
By Your own working, Lord, empower
Till Satan's forts we storm.

Help each of us to do our part;
O Lord, may we not fail.
Give clearest guidance to each heart
Till highest mounts we scale.
Use us however You may choose;
We would no burden, Lord, refuse;

But get us, Lord, where You can use
And mightily prevail.

Oh, send the promised Holy Ghost
Upon us as we kneel,
We need His holy working most
Till men conviction feel.
Lord, this is still the day of grace;
Have mercy on our dying race.
Revival send to every place;
Your miracle reveal.

—*Wesley Duewel*[5]

Oswald Chambers ———

Surrounded by God's Presence

TRUSTING GOD FOR EVERYTHING

Oswald Chambers was born in a Baptist minister's home in Aberdeen, Scotland, on July 24, 1874. He was one of the nine children of Clarence and Hannah Chambers, both of whom were baptized by Charles Spurgeon. Later Clarence entered pastors' college and was ordained a Baptist minister by Spurgeon.

As a child Oswald had a beautiful faith and trust in his heavenly Father. To the end of his life he remained childlike in faith and simplicity. In a very natural way he asked God for things and expected God's answer. When he went upstairs to bed each evening, he would pray. His family members often would stand on the stairs to listen to him pray. Whether he asked for guinea pigs in his childhood, or for a specific book he needed in his library as a young man, or for railway fare or passage money to Japan as an adult, Oswald simply asked God to answer and expected the result.

When Oswald was seven years old, he began attending school, where he developed his natural gift for drawing. This became his main school joy. When Oswald was twelve, he and his father were walking home one night after hearing Spurgeon preach, and Oswald told his father that if Spurgeon had given an invitation, he would have given himself to the Lord.

"You can do it now, my boy," his father replied.

Right there in the street Oswald was saved and from then on lived for his Lord. Soon he was baptized and joined the Baptist church. Shortly thereafter he began to teach a Sunday school class.

Two YMCA workers took Oswald along with them to visit lodging houses where poor workmen lived. From then on Oswald gave much of his time to doing evangelism among these people, some of whom were ex-convicts. When Oswald was eighteen, he enrolled in an art school in London and received the Art Master's Certificate, which licensed him to teach art and earn his livelihood by art.

In 1895 Oswald returned to Scotland and took an arts course at Edinburgh University. He began a friendship with Gertrude Hobbs, who years later became his wife. They took many walks, discussing the relation of Christian life to art, music, and poetry.

(The Christian world is greatly indebted to Gertrude—whom Oswald called "Biddy"—who over the years kept a complete and careful shorthand record of his sermons, classes, and correspondence. She drew upon those for all his books, which she prepared after his untimely death. Her biography gathers many of these incidents and quotes.)[1]

CALL TO MINISTRY

One night as Oswald prayed on a hillside, he heard the audible voice of God say, "I want you in My service—but I can do without you." So unmistakably clear was God's call to him that at once he determined to give up his art career and obey God. He wrote to his father, telling him that he was enrolling in college to prepare for the ministry. His father was delighted.

In 1897, at the age of twenty-three, Oswald enrolled in the College of Dunoon (Scotland), a small Baptist college run by faith principles. College officials told no one their needs. Whenever food was not in supply, faculty and students together searched their hearts to see who had grieved the Lord or why the funds had not come in. This principle was in full harmony with Oswald's own life of prayer and faith.

Oswald wrote to his father, "I am not good nor worthy, nor do I think I am, but the ring of my Master's passion is in my soul, and I am impelled by the insistent mercy and love of God. How can I disobey His voice, so clear to my own convictions?"

LESSONS IN FAITH

While at the college Oswald became a close friend of William Quarrier, founder of a faith ministry, orphanage, and tuberculosis sanitorium in Glasgow. Eventually Quarrier's ministries grew until more than fifteen hundred children were being cared for in three locations in Scotland and Canada. On Friday nights Oswald and Quarrier would pray together for the funds Quarrier needed for the next week without telling anyone of the need or using fund-raising schemes. Oswald learned to trust God for all his needs.

Oswald stayed at the training college for nine years, becoming a part-time lecturer in his second year and becoming a regular tutor thereafter. He testified that from the time of his new birth as a boy he "enjoyed the presence of Jesus Christ wonderfully, but years passed before I gave myself up thoroughly to His work."

Oswald's niece described how he adapted to children: "He used to take family prayers with us in the evenings before we went to bed, and his prayers were just like natural talks to a beloved father. The naturalness of his religion impressed us children. He never had any other manner for Sundays or the pulpit, or for any other occasion or any person. . . .

"If he wanted to give a word of advice, he would use some catchy hymn tune we all knew and make up appropriate words to it. One day when I, the only daughter, failed to do an obvious domestic duty, he suddenly lifted up his voice and sang, to a familiar tune:

> It's better to shine than to whine,
> It's better now than before,
> It's better to wash the tea things up
> Than sulk by the kitchen door!"[2]

FILLED WITH THE SPIRIT

While Oswald was a tutor at Dunoon College, Dr. F. B. Meyer came and spoke about the role of the Holy Spirit in the believer. Oswald said, "I determined to have all that was going and went to my room and asked God simply and definitely for the baptism of the Holy Spirit, whatever that meant." In the next four years God used Oswald in the conversion of others. But in his own heart Oswald still was not satisfied.

"The last three months of those years things reached a climax. I was getting very desperate. . . . Then Luke 11:13 got hold of me. . . . God brings one to the point of utter despair." At a small meeting while the congregation was singing a chorus, by naked faith Oswald claimed the fullness of the Spirit. He felt no dramatic change but knew he had trusted God.

Oswald was asked to speak at a meeting, and at the close forty people came forward to seek the Lord. He was so terrified at what had happened that he walked out of the room and went to the Reverend McGregor, the principal of Dunoon College.

McGregor asked Oswald, "Don't you remember claiming the Holy Spirit as a gift on the word of Jesus, and that He said, 'Ye shall receive power...'? This is the power from on high."

Oswald wrote, "These five years have truly been heaven on earth. Glory be to God, the last aching abyss of the human heart is filled to overflowing with the love of God. Love is the beginning, love is the middle, and love is the end. After He comes in, all you see is 'Jesus only, Jesus ever.' When you know what God has done for you, the power and the tyranny of sin are gone and the radiant unspeakable emancipation of the indwelling Christ has come."

INTERNATIONAL MINISTRY

In 1905 Oswald met Bishop Juji Nakada, cofounder with Charles Cowman of the work of the Oriental Missionary Society (now called OMS International) in Japan. They shared the same vision and teamed up to conduct meetings for Christian holiness in various parts of the British Isles. Nakada convinced Oswald to accompany him to the United States to conduct camp meetings and conventions.

Nakada described the prayer life of Oswald Chambers: "He was a wonderful man of prayer. Though the sea was rough, yet lying there on his berth, he turned the leaves of his book which contained the names of those he prayed for, and day or night he never ceased praying and interceding for them even though at times he did not feel too good."[3] Oswald once wrote in his diary, "I do believe that this is where my real ministry lies—in intercessory prayer."

Oswald and Nakada made God's Bible School and Missionary Training Home in Cincinnati, Ohio, their headquarters in the United States, and Oswald taught there for several months. Here he met the Cowmans, who with Nakada had begun a seminary and missionary work in Tokyo. Later Oswald made the Tokyo OMS Bible Seminary, which the Cowmans and Nakada had founded, his Japan headquarters. God made Oswald a great blessing in Japan and gave him a missionary vision.

THE SENSE OF GOD'S PRESENCE

Oswald wrote from Cincinnati on February 4, 1907, "We have had some blessed times already here. God is so near that at times the blessing of our Father is more than one can bear. Have you ever felt it? I have no difficulty in seeing how the saints will meet the Lord in the air, for when the Lord blesses so much here, and your physical frame seems incandescent with God's fire—why, it is just a wonder you don't rise, and when He comes we shall all be changed in the twinkling of an eye."[4]

On February 16, 1907, Oswald wrote, "As we obey the leadings of the Spirit of God, we enable God to answer the prayers of other people. I mean that our lives, my life, is the answer to someone's prayer, prayed perhaps centuries ago. . . . I have the unspeakable knowledge that my life is the answer to prayers, and that God is blessing me and making me a blessing entirely of His sovereign grace and nothing to do with my merits, except as I am bold enough to trust His leading and not the dictates of my own wisdom and common sense. The sense of 'my Father' has been wonderful lately. The access in prayer is so ineffably sweet and natural, I am just flooded with a deep settled peace in my soul."[5]

Wrote one friend, "To hear him pray was to be in the presence of God. Like Murray McCheyne and Samuel Rutherford, he seemed to live in uninterrupted communion with God." Another wrote of his "spiritual incandescence derived from living continuously in the presence of God."[6]

THE ANOINTING OF THE SPIRIT

On April 7, 1907, Oswald wrote, "We had a grand day yesterday. God comes on you in the hour of preaching in an unspeakable manner. Yesterday God laid hold of me and I uttered things that amazed me even while I spoke. I could see what God was evidently working in my heart and soul. Oh, for more and mightier power for God! It is a zeal that eats me up." Then on April 19 he wrote, "This has been a blessed day. My room has been the resort of the heavy-laden and the sin-stricken. I am overwhelmed before our Lord. They come, and nothing but the Spirit of God could draw them. Crying in tears and blessed rejoicing. It is an unspeakably blessed thing to see souls come out under the blessing of the baptism of the Holy Ghost and fire. Some simply laugh, peels of heartiest and most blessed laughter you ever heard, just a modern edition of 'then was our mouth filled with laughter.'" And, "What woes, what burdens people carry. I was impressed to give a Bible reading on 'The Discipline of Suffering' on Sunday, and God gave me a blessed time in my own soul."[7]

Oswald recorded on May 6, "We had a blessedly wonderful day yesterday. We went into the tabernacle on the hill at 10:30 A.M. and did not leave until 5:00 P.M. Many souls cut loose; there were tears and laughter and all the blessed signs of those revival times the Lord brings so mysteriously and suddenly upon His people. It is a great business to open up all the windows of the soul to heaven and live on the hallelujah side. Oh, it's blessed to find people all over this vast continent hungry for God."

The next day Oswald penned, "This morning I went to conduct a prayer meeting at nine o'clock and have just left it, five o'clock and it is still in full swing. . . . simply one huge altar service all the time, no addresses and no hymns, just prayer and confessing and getting right with God. Blessed be God, He can dig souls out right gloriously. It is a blessed and glorious work. You forget all about breakfast and dinner two days running. I forgot all about my dinner for prayer and rejoicing. Fasting is a glorious job when you don't even know you do it. These are memorable seasons."[8]

In Japan with OMS

On July 10, 1907, Nakada took Oswald on board the *Empress of Japan* to sail for Japan. On July 27 they landed in Yokohama harbor, where Charles Cowman and E. A. Kilbourne were waiting to take Oswald to the OMS Bible school. He was overwhelmed with the organization and extent of the OMS work, the godliness of the Japanese coworkers, and the wonderful meetings he shared. He wrote, "The whole thing has so absorbed and enthralled me that I have been like the Queen of Sheba. The work is absorbing. I do not know what I expected, but I never expected such an elaborate, splendidly organized work as it is."[9]

Oswald wrote his brother Franklin, "I never imagined or saw anything quite like it. Nakada is a mighty preacher here. To see the altar service is wonderful. They come out fifty to a hundred, without any persuasion, and then the work begins. Every worker gets on his knees with his Bible and instruction goes on for hours, for they know nothing of the Christian revelation; they will stay all night, and when they do get through it is wonderful. God puts His seal on these people as He rarely seems to do in the homeland (Britain) or America. Their faith is marvelous and God answers it, but it is simply too baffling to try and speak of it all."[10]

After a blessed time in Japan, Oswald took the Cowmans with him, and they all sailed for Britain. Oswald introduced the Cowmans to God's people in that land, especially to the leaders and people of the League of Prayer, which had such a tremendous influence on Oswald's life, bringing him into the light and experience of holiness of heart. This led to establishing the British Isles base for OMS International. OMS has maintained a British Isles partnership since that time.

LIFE IN THE FULLNESS OF THE SPIRIT

For the next several years Oswald traveled to the United States during the summertime to speak in Bible schools and camp meetings. An English minister wrote of his meeting with Oswald and Nakada: "The joy in both their faces is a benediction still as I think of them. The outstanding impression of that great meeting was Mr. Chambers' own testimony. He reminded you of the Apostle Paul, a teacher and leader of the first rank. It was Oswald Chambers who led me more deeply into the meaning of the cross."[11]

Of those days Rosa Gardener wrote, "Every recollection of Oswald Chambers is of a man indwelt by the Holy Spirit and always, all the time, in love with his Master."[12]

A Miss Carrier said, "On Sunday after lunch Mr. Chambers said he would take ten minutes' sleep before the afternoon service. I said, 'You seem very sure of sleeping; will you want rousing?' In his decided manner he said, 'Of course I shall sleep, I'm going to ask my heavenly Father for ten minutes' sleep, and He will rouse me on the tick of the clock.' Needless to say, it was exactly so! He was sure of God and witnessed to it sleeping and waking."[13]

HUNGER FOR THE SPIRIT'S TOUCH

Oswald longed for deep spiritual reality. He said, "I see churches and schemes and missionary enterprises, and holiness movements, all tagged with His name, and how little of Himself! I wish every breath I drew, all speech I made, could make Him come and seem more real to men. Nothing is worth living for but just Himself. . . . I am hungry with a vast desire for Him . . . the call is on me, intolerably strong at times."

Oswald hungered for spiritual results from his ministry. On January 8, 1909, he recorded, "I feel as if living is impossible if He does not save and sanctify souls through me. . . . If I could only tell Him as I know Him . . . the loveliness of our Lord comes home to me more and more. How few of us are concerned about satisfying His heart. How I hear Him saying, 'Give me to drink.' May my Lord never let me grow cold in my longing to be a cup in His hand for the quenching of His royal thirst. I have only one absorbing interest, and that is that He gets His way.... More and more it is only Himself, not evangelism, but just Himself and obedience to Him. I seek loyalty to Him and nothing else."[14]

LIFE IN GOD'S PRESENCE

John Thatcher of Inverness, a friend of Oswald's, wrote, "To hear [Oswald] pray was to be in the presence of God. Like Murray McCheyne and Samuel Rutherford, he seemed to live in uninterrupted communion with God."[15]

Oswald entered this on December 15, 1908: "My Lord Jesus Christ grows grander, and more and more central to my mind and heart and being daily."[16]

Mrs. Howard Hooker noted, "For six months before his marriage in 1910 Oswald Chambers made our home his headquarters. During this time he was a great inspiration both to my husband and to myself. His ideals were terrific, but he lived up to them.... He was a man who always carried with him, and therefore gave to others, a sense of the presence of God. We noticed this in his merriest moments as well as in his ordinary life, or in the most serious part of his ministry. We loved having him in our home. He taught us so much. He played with our children, and was never happier than when crawling around the nursery playing at being a lion or a tiger, led triumphantly by a small boy or girl whom he allowed to tease him unmercifully."[17]

PRINCIPAL OF DUNOON COLLEGE

After his marriage, Oswald served as principal of the College of Dunoon from January 1911 to July 1915. The school sought to help all its students live Oswald's long-standing motto, "My utmost for His highest." One of his students wrote, "His life was truly Spirit-filled, and the one burning passion was devotion to his Savior. Continually in his lectures he pressed home the importance of 'personal, passionate devotion to Jesus Christ,' and the necessity of maintaining our relationship to Him at any cost. This was the secret of his own power in the service for God. He lived the Sermon on the Mount."[18]

Another student remarked, "[Chambers] was a man of prayer, and the atmosphere of the whole college was charged with the presence of God."

Another had this to say: "Elisha is referred to as 'the man of God,' and Mr. Chambers was such a man to me always.... One of the outstanding impressions of those days was the terrifically high standard put before us, nothing less than our all and our utmost would suffice."

One student recalled, "The thing that struck me most of all in Mr. Chambers' life, and which grows on me since his death, is that he never left you with the sense of himself as predominate, but always with his Lord and Master. He led you to a deeper knowledge of Jesus Christ.... One incident of many comes to my mind and illustrates what he so often said—that a disciple of our Lord should have a family likeness to Him. Walking with him one evening through a little country village, he just very naturally stopped and prayed, asking for God's blessing on the village, and it seemed so like what our Lord would have done when He was on earth."[19]

Another wrote, "As one entered the room it was like stepping into heaven. Then Mr. Chambers spoke, leading us straight to God, and I afterwards found that this was very characteristic of him. In every lecture or meeting he brought one right into the presence of God."

MINISTRY IN EGYPT

In 1915 the Bible college closed for what officials thought would be the war's duration. Oswald offered to go to Egypt with the allied forces as a chaplain in the YMCA work. For two years he labored among the servicemen in desert camps of the Egyptian expeditionary force.

The YMCA huts Oswald had built in the desert sand were a home away from home for soldiers who could get away for a few hours, purchase refreshments, and write letters home. And in the evenings they would come and listen to Oswald lecture. The soldiers were under no pressure to attend, but men constantly came to sit at Oswald's feet in his Bible studies and lectures. In front, a small tent was pitched, where morning after morning he went to be alone with God. From 5:30 until 7:30 A.M. was his time alone with God in prayer. "It was there he gained the radiance that shone from his face, and the message sharper than any two-edged sword that pierced through every veil to the dividing asunder of the joints and marrow."[20]

Time and again when someone would say, "That cannot be done," Oswald would say, "Let's pray about it," and soon the problem would be solved on their knees. His diary of October 13, 1915, included these words: "There is scarcely an hour in which I do not adore God for His wonderful reality to me, and for the complete realization that I do not deserve it. . . . Truly His will is the gladdest, finest thing conceivable."

Oswald felt that his great work in Egypt was intercession. On October 8, 1916, he wrote, "It is more and more impressed upon me that prayer is *the* work, that the discovery of God's truth and the deliverance of souls is wrought by preaching and by prayer in implicit faith on the ground of redemption." He later recorded, "*Intercession* was the great word with which God called me out, and it is emphasized again."

THE PRESENCE OF ANGELS

Oswald was at times very aware of the presence of angels. While traveling to America by ship on November 11, 1906, he wrote, "Probably the most persistent sentiment with me is the watch of the angel hosts in answer to the prayers of the numerous saints in the homeland. It seems to me as if a special watch surrounded this boat. I seem to hear them in the rolling air, and to feel their touches even through my whole body."

On December 3, 1916, in Egypt, Oswald recorded, "As I walked through the lines tonight, alone in this mighty desert, under the serene dome of the sky and the wonderful stars, I realized again the unique sense of the presence of angels. I noticed it repeatedly the first time I went abroad. It is quite distinct from the certainty that God is guarding; this is the beautiful sense of angel presence. Anyway that is how it strikes me, and I thank God for it."[21]

SUDDEN ILLNESS AND DEATH

In the autumn of 1917, General Allenby was preparing to make his last advance and to capture Jerusalem, and Oswald was preparing to go with the troops. He was stricken with appendicitis, which was wrongly diagnosed, and he died of peritonitis on November 15, 1917, at age forty-three.

Yet his ministry lived on because his wife turned her voluminous shorthand notes into many books, which have blessed people around the world. She wrote, "His writings were only an outpouring of a passion for holiness and an intense intimate relationship with the Lord."

The bishop of Salisbury, the Right Reverend J. E. Fison, said of Oswald, "It is impressive to see in Oswald Chambers a man who experienced a most definite 'second blessing' of sanctification, and yet passed on, not to deny the crucial importance of Luke 11:13, 'If ye then, being evil, know how to give good gifts unto your children, how much more shall your heavenly Father give the Holy Spirit to them that ask him?'—a text which he always kept on using in personal work—but to an ever greater faith in and reliance upon the inexhaustible riches of the person of our Lord."[22]

Fison further said, "God gave him complete freedom and yet in every detail of daily life unceasingly cared for him. He reflected his Master's voice. Again and again he reverts to the sparrows and the lilies, and in the spirit of Matthew 6:25 he comes out with the emphatic 'I *refuse* to worry.' That is what kept his own spirit so childlike and boyish in all his dealings with the troops in Egypt."[23]

Oswald's body was laid to rest with military honors among the soldiers' graves at Old Cairo. "A believer in Jesus Christ" is the inscription on the tomb, his own description of himself. In addition are these words from Luke 11:13: "How much more will your heavenly Father give the Holy Spirit to them that ask him?"[24]

Oswald had lived out day by day the title of his best-known book, *My Utmost for His Highest*.

In one of his early poems Oswald wrote:

> Dearer than all that is nearest,
> Dearer than dear, or than dearest,
> Dearer than sight,
> Dearer than light,
> Is the communion with Jesus.[25]

Jonathan Goforth ———

Man of Revival

A Youth on Fire for God

Jonathan Goforth was born near London, Ontario, Canada, on February 10, 1859. He was born again at the age of eighteen, and he immediately sought ways to serve the Lord. Every Sunday morning he would stand at the church door and give each person a gospel tract. And he started Sunday evening services in an old schoolhouse at an early age.

In his youth Jonathan felt called to the ministry, and for two years before he entered Knox College in Toronto to prepare for the ministry, he got up two hours early each morning to find time for unbroken Bible study. His Bible was his most precious possession, and he read it through again and again.

From the time he heard his first missionary speaker, Jonathan felt called to be a missionary and began to read everything he could find about missions and also sought to give others a missionary vision.

When he entered Knox College, Jonathan was greatly disappointed and shocked to find that others were not seeking to be soul winners and laughed at the stories of his attempts to win prostitutes and other sinners in the slums. His very first Sunday in college he began jail ministry. At times he did not have enough money to buy a postage stamp, but he learned to trust God for his needs.

Throughout his college years Jonathan ministered in the slums, house to house, sometimes leading two or three to Christ in one afternoon. He evangelized in seventeen brothels on one street, leading many young prostitutes to Christ. One summer he evangelized 960 homes.

Jonathan's first preaching assignment was to an area twenty-two miles long and twelve miles wide, with four preaching points. He visited every home in the area. Soon the buildings where services were held were too small to hold all the people.

During this time Jonathan met his future wife, Rosalind, who was also involved in city mission work in Toronto.

CANADIAN PRESBYTERIANS ENTER CHINA

Jonathan's denomination, the Canadian Presbyterian Church, had no work in China and no plans to open work there, so Jonathan decided he would have to go under the China Inland Mission. His fellow students in college, however, thought he should go with his own denomination and voted unanimously to support him. He bought hundreds of copies of a book on China by Hudson Taylor and mailed them to Presbyterian ministers. In June 1888 the Presbyterian Church of Canada voted to open up work in China, and Jonathan was appointed along with another person to be part of the first party.

In October, just after Jonathan was ordained, he married Rosalind Bell-Smith. The Goforths sailed on February 4, 1888, to China from Vancouver. Jonathan's heart longed for souls, and he began to pray for ten thousand Chinese souls. They proceeded to Chefoo (now called Yantai) in China and immediately plunged into language study. The second week they were there their house burned down and most of their belongings were destroyed.

In September Jonathan accompanied a missionary of another society to make an inspection trip into south Honan (Henan) province, where they felt God was leading them. China Inland

Mission had tried unsuccessfully for ten years to enter that province, and Hudson Taylor wrote Jonathan, "Brother, if you would enter that province, you must go forward on your knees."[1] These words became the slogan of Jonathan and his group as they entered north Honan.

In July of 1889 dysentery broke out. Several people died, including baby Gertrude Goforth. Jonathan had to travel fifty miles to find a cemetery where foreigners could be buried. (Gertrude was the first of eleven children, five of whom died as infants.) Soon a son, Donald, was born into their home, and he died at nineteen months after a fall from a veranda.

GOD'S HELP WITH LANGUAGE

Month after month Jonathan studied the difficult Chinese language, but language had always been difficult for him. He made embarrassingly small progress, and the Chinese would say they could not understand him when he preached. Suddenly, one day while he was trying to preach, words, phrases, and idioms began to flood through his mind, and he was able to make himself understood. Later he found that a group of students at Knox College had gone into a room to pray just for him. They all felt God's presence in a tremendous way and were sure God had done something for Jonathan. Jonathan became very fluent in the language from that time on.

ESCAPE FROM A MOB

Soon Jonathan had a narrow escape from a wild mob, the first of many. For months he had great difficulty in getting people to listen to him, because false stories were circulated and notices put up by government officials warning people that the missionaries kidnapped small children and took out their eyes and hearts and made them into powerful medicine.

Finally, Jonathan appealed to the British government minister at Peking (Beijing), and he contacted Chinese authorities to stop this circulation of lies about the missionaries. Proclamations were posted throughout the villages telling people these foreigners were there by treaty right and anyone molesting them would be duly punished. This helped bring a change of attitude. Nevertheless, Jonathan often had to stand with his back to a wall so that people wouldn't attack him from behind. The living conditions in the village where the Goforths were located were very poor, but that was the only place they could find to stay.

MOVE TO CHANGTE

After two years the missionaries felt God wanted them in the central city of Changte (Changde), and by 1894 permission was granted. Within twenty-four hours of reaching the city, they received thirty-two offers of property, including the very place they desired. But that summer the whole area was flooded with six to eight feet of water, and almost all of the Goforths' possessions were destroyed.

FIRST CHINESE COWORKER

For almost seven years Jonathan and Rosalind had been praying and believing they would be able to begin work in Changte. They worked night and day, nearly to exhaustion. Jonathan asked God to supply someone to help in the chapel preaching. The next day a converted opium addict arrived dressed in rags. He was emaciated and ghastly pale. He and his family had been eating leaves to survive. Jonathan immediately ordered a good meal for the man, whose name was Wang Fulin. Could this be the answer to their prayers? Within an hour or two the ragged beggar was clean and dressed in one of Jonathan's outfits. From the very first day, the Goforths sensed the power of the Spirit anointing the former addict.

Jonathan and Wang Fulin preached an average of eight hours a day. The former addict testified to how God had delivered him from opium. People would often sit as much as half a day listening to the messages, and many were convicted of their sins. Jonathan experienced unusual anointings of the Holy Spirit, and the power of the Lord was on him more than ever before.

Daily Holy Spirit Enablement

In April 1896 Jonathan wrote that in the past five months he had experienced daily manifestations of the Holy Spirit's power. At least twenty-five thousand men and women heard the gospel preached, and the preaching continued for an average of eight hours a day. Sometimes fifty or more women were in the yard at the same time listening to Rosalind. Often as many as ten to twenty of them were moved upon by the Spirit and sought salvation.

"Open House"

By the fall of 1897 the Goforths had finished building a more adequate home. It looked Chinese on the outside but Canadian on the inside. The Chinese were amazed at wooden floors, glass windows, foreign furniture, an organ, a sewing machine (which they called an iron tailor), and even a pump to bring water from the well without a bucket. They called little Paul's tricycle a "self-propelled cart." Crowds of people came to see the building and its amazing contents. Paul, child number 3, would demonstrate riding his tricycle around the yard. Florence, number 4, would wheel baby Helen back and forth in a baby carriage. A few times, to the amazement of the people, Jonathan insisted that if they wanted to see the house and its contents, they had to be willing to stand and listen to the gospel. Visitors stole anything they could lay their hands on and slipped it up their big sleeves.

The greatest attendance was on a day in 1899 when 1,835 men passed through the house and Rosalind received about 500 women. Jonathan preached until nightfall. He announced he would admit 150 at a time, but before he could stop them, 500 would come in. Rosalind usually demonstrated the organ. But one day she was so busy Jonathan had to demonstrate it himself. Not being able to play, he just pressed his hands down on as many keys as possible and pumped the bellows at full strength. The Chinese were absolutely delighted and said, "He plays better than his wife."

God used the Goforths' hospitality to break down prejudice and convince the Chinese the missionaries had nothing dangerous hidden in the house. Their "open house" policy opened many doors for them, and people would say, "We were at your house, and you showed us through your house and treated us like we were your friends." Then they would bring out a chair for Jonathan to sit on and a table to put his Bible on, and they would often serve him tea.

Ruth Isabel, child number 7, arrived on New Year's Day 1898. In October 1899, Grace Muriel, child number 6, who had been ill for over a year with what finally proved to be pernicious malaria and an enlarged spleen, died in her father's arms, having just looked into his face and smiled. Mother Rosalind was on her knees in the next room praying that Gracie would not die in convulsions as their children Gertrude and Donald had.

The next day Paul was found to be seriously ill with measles and dysentery, but God spared his life. For weeks Jonathan himself lay seriously ill with a bad attack of jaundice, and Rosalind almost died of exhaustion and illness.

Yet night after night people gathered to hear the gospel message. When the missionaries would stop preaching, the people would call out, often a hundred or two hundred at the same time, "Stay. Tell us more." By May of 1900 Christian communities had been started in more than fifty villages.

MIRACLE DELIVERANCE FROM THE BOXERS

The turn of the century brought the dreadful Boxer Rebellion in China, a militant antiforeign movement built up with resentment to the Opium War of 1839–42, which had been provoked by Britain and had involved forcing China to make concessions. The Chinese resented European and Western influence and especially Britain, France, Germany, and Russia. The Roman Catholic religion was also strongly resented. The rebellion finally resulted in an antiforeign secret society called in English "The Boxers."

In June 1900 the Boxers occupied Peking, and for eight weeks they besieged foreigners and Chinese Christians until defeated and the siege was lifted by an international force of British, French, Russian, American, German, and Japanese troops. Rioting occurred in many parts of China. America insisted the Chinese territorial and administrative entity be preserved, though China was forced to pay an indemnity to the foreign nations. The United States used part of its share for scholarships for Chinese students.

The Christians were the main ones who suffered in the Boxer Rebellion. Hundreds of Roman Catholic chapels and Protestant churches were destroyed. In the rioting at least five Roman Catholic bishops, 311 priests, and probably more than 30,000 Roman Catholic members were killed.[2] Thousands more were tortured.

At least 108 Protestant missionaries (including twenty-one from the Christian and Missionary Alliance and eleven from the China Inland Mission) and more than 300 children of missionaries were killed.[3] It is against this background that we must picture the miracle of God's protection and deliverance of the Goforth group.

Here is the story. Daughter Florence, who was seven years old, contracted meningitis and died on June 19, 1900. Almost immediately, two messages from the American Consul at Chefoo—which had been delayed some days—arrived, ordering them to flee south. A party of three missionary men, five women, four children, and three servants started out on June 27 in a springless wooden cart on what promised to be a ten-day escape journey. They faced angry mobs shouting, "Kill! Kill!" and a fusillade of stones and firing of guns.

Jonathan shouted, "Take everything but don't kill." His left arm was slashed several times by a sword, his pith helmet was almost slashed to pieces, and one sword blow came a fraction of an inch from slashing his skull. A blow knocked him to the ground, but just then he heard a clear voice, probably an angel, which said, "Fear not, they are praying for you."[4]

Just as he was losing consciousness, Jonathan saw a horse galloping toward him. When he regained consciousness, the horse had fallen and was kicking so furiously that it drove the crowd back. A crowd of thousands began to loot the carts and fought each other to get the loot. Rosalind's shoes were pulled off and stolen. Again the Goforth parents were stoned.

The missionaries reached a village where they were given a room, and they bandaged their wounds. Nine of them crowded on a cart that had held three before. When they reached a larger town, they were again stoned but reached an inn. The mob shouted, "Kill! Kill!" After an hour or two the mob demanded that they line up on the narrow veranda outside their room. They were insulted and jeered at, but not a weapon was used against them.

A few soldiers were sent to take the missionaries to a place of great danger. However, the soldiers climbed on the carts, and they and the carters fell asleep, and the animals went the wrong way. When the soldiers awoke, they were far from where they had wanted to be, but this saved the lives of the party. At least a dozen times that day they were stopped by wild mobs but escaped and went on.

They reached another walled city and met another mob, but just then two well-dressed young Chinese officials pushed through the crowd, recognized Jonathan, and persuaded the mob that these were good foreigners. The two young officials provided them with anti-septic bandages and a one-man escort to lead them out of the area. The missionaries were almost dead with exhaustion but pressed on another twenty hours. They were able to get on boats, which took them to Shanghai, where they were put on a ship to Canada.

After a few months' ministry in Canada, word came to the Goforths that some missionaries were starting back to reopen North China. Jonathan left his family and went back. In May 1902 he sent for his family. On July 1 Rosalind took their five children (Paul, Helen, Ruth, William, and Amelia), ages ten years to eight months, and started back to China. Jonathan was going to meet them in Shanghai, but he became terribly ill with typhoid in the interior. One day, after a two-week journey, he finally arrived, a shadow of his old self, as he had lost so much weight.

Jonathan took his family by houseboat up the river. Then they went overland by cart again. He felt led to open a new station, but Rosalind refused for the sake of the children—they had already buried four other children in China. Jonathan insisted they would be safest in God's will.

Two of the children came down with dysentery. William recovered, but Amelia did not. Nevertheless, the Goforths began a heavy schedule of meetings and began planting churches.

About 1904, an unknown British family sent them several pamphlets on the Welsh revival. God gave Jonathan a vision of revival for China. A missionary friend in India sent him a pamphlet that contained part of Charles Finney's lectures on revival. Jonathan said, "If Finney is right, and I believe he is, I am going to find out what those laws [of revival] are and obey them regardless of the cost."[5] He sent to Canada for three books on prayer and revival, one being the full *Finney's Lectures on Revival*.

God began to give a touch of revival in China, and it burgeoned. In 1907 Jonathan was chosen to accompany the secretary of the Canadian Presbyterian Home Board of Missions who was visiting China. Jonathan traveled with him to Korea to check on reports of revival in the Presbyterian work there. The Welsh revival had leaped to India among the Welsh Presbyterian work and then from India to Korea. They found that the revival exceeded the reports they had received.

When Jonathan returned to China, wherever he went he told the story of revival in Korea. At each place he was requested to come back and hold a ten-day revival mission. Yet it was nearly a year before he could return. When he did, God led him to (1) tell the story of Korea and the revival, (2) preach on the Holy Spirit, and (3) make the cross of Jesus Christ central. His watchword was, "Not by might, nor by power, but by my spirit" (Zech. 4:6). God so blessed Jonathan's ministry in Manchuria that requests for ministry began to come from many parts of China and from different missionary societies.

The next year, Jonathan's presbytery decided to free him for revival work full-time for a while, and Rosalind prepared to take the children to Canada during this special time of his ministry. She asked her husband, "If I suddenly was faced with an incurable disease and we cabled you to come, would you come?"

Jonathan reluctantly replied that he hoped this issue would never need to be faced.

She insisted: "Would you?"

After some thought, he replied, "If our nation were at war with another nation and I was in charge of an important unit in the Army, would I be permitted to leave my unit for family reasons?"

"No," she answered, "king and country would come first."

He reminded her that when they married they had promised to put God first in their relationship.

Within a week Rosalind and the six children (including number 10 Mary and number 11 Johyn) left for Canada.

God used Jonathan mightily in place after place. His ministry was primarily to begin with the church. In Changte, after several messages, one man began to pray. Within moments one after another began to call on God for mercy. In moments the whole group was calling to God for mercy and forgiveness. It was like a sudden thunderstorm of prayer. In service after service, morning, afternoon, and night, God took over the services and people confessed their spiritual needs, and person after person received pardon, purity, and power.

Prayer meetings were held before the general meetings and between services. And during those days prayer after prayer was answered. Near the end of the ten days of meetings, the meetings lasted almost all day with only brief breaks for food. Missionaries and Chinese, pastors and people—all were humbling themselves, calling on God for forgiveness and mercy. Hundreds were attending the services and were sending messages to people in nearby towns urging them to come too. Release and liberty of heart resulted in joy-filled countenances. Everyone was overflowing with love for everyone else. Missionary to missionary, Chinese to Chinese, and missionary to Chinese—all were one in Christ Jesus.

Early in 1909, right after wonderful meetings in the Peking area, Jonathan left for Britain, where the China Inland Mission had arranged general meetings in London. He was taken to see an invalid Christian woman who was known to be a great intercessor. She told how when he began meetings in Manchuria she had heard about it and had since been interceding for him. She handed him her prayer notebook and told him of three special occasions when God had enabled her to prevail mightily in intercession for him. As Jonathan looked at the dates in the notebook, he was deeply moved to discover that these were the three times God had worked in tremendous might and power in Manchuria![6]

Jonathan's furlough year in Canada had some gracious services but on the whole was disappointing to him. He did not find the spiritual hunger, the openness to revival, or the welcome to his reports that he had hoped for. On the way back to China he had special conferences in Northern Ireland, ten days at Charles Spurgeon's tabernacle in London, and a week as one of the speakers at the Keswick Convention. The Keswick executive asked him to give a year to ministry in Britain under their auspices. When Jonathan cabled his presbytery in China for permission, they told him his field was in China.

Jonathan longed for Chinese evangelists to help in the work, prayed for them, and prayed in the funds for them since the mission board would not increase the budget. The Goforths returned with joy to their station and ministry. He labored incessantly until for a period of three months he had a series of carbuncles and abscesses. The doctor told Jonathan he was headed for the grave unless he took some rest. He returned to Canada.

In 1917 Jonathan returned to China to devote part time to his station work and part time to revival ministries. Liberalism and modernism became an issue, so Jonathan resigned from his mission board. They generously permitted him to move to another location, and Goforths' home was taken over by a board replacement.

For two years Goforth moved from place to place about every five days. He spoke to Christian and Missionary Alliance missionaries on the Spirit-filled life and went wherever he was invited. Then came an invitation to hold spiritual life meetings for Christian General Feng Yuhsiang's army. Jonathan spoke to about one thousand each day. The marshall wept as he prayed for them and the country. One after another of his officers prayed and wept for China. God gave great meetings during the year Jonathan spent working with the soldiers of General Feng's army.

When the 1920 famine came to north-central China, more than $120,000 in relief funds raised through the Goforths was forwarded to the needy. And more than three thousand Chinese were won to the Lord. But Rosalind also became very ill. The Goforth team consisted of Rosalind in a chair as her husband walked beside her, the evangelists, three Bible women, and pack animals with bedding. This was their procession from place to place. The area was too rough for carts. School boys with patriotic caps led the way. Street vendors would rise and stand at attention until the procession passed by. In places where they had been insulted during the Boxer Rebellion they were now honored. They had large attentive day audiences and crowds at night. Thousands heard the gospel in those days.

Jonathan returned on furlough to Canada, only to find the church was in a crisis hour over the issue of church union, so he spent the summer in missionary gatherings and conventions in the United States.

Jonathan was nearly sixty-eight when his mission commissioned him to return to China to open a new field. Rosalind needed medical attention but could not get it for several days, so they started back to China anyway. In the next six months, five times the door of a promising field shut in their faces. But at last the door to Manchuria opened. The two Goforths, two single women, and a new young man established a field in Szepingkai. They began with preaching seminars seven hours a day. They had a Chinese coworker and one other loaned to them. During the first month about two hundred Chinese made decisions for Christ.[7]

Jonathan had to have his teeth extracted by a Japanese dentist but caught cold in his lower jaw with serious complications. For four months he could not go to the chapel. His son Fred came to China and typed the stories Jonathan told, thus completing the book *By My Spirit*.

By now Jonathan had appointed thirty evangelists to help on the field. He solicited no funds but trusted the Lord for funds to support them. The mission had no financial aid for the new work, but in 1930 when the mission asked the Goforths to return to

Canada for furlough and for medical care for Rosalind, God sent them money, which they used to support their Chinese coworkers while they were gone.

During the furlough Jonathan had to have repeated eye operations for cataracts. Nevertheless, he returned to Manchuria and held revival campaigns in center after center. For six months in 1932 he held revival meetings in many parts of the China field. He had tremendous meetings in Changte, where he and his family had spent so many years. Then in March 1933 the retina in his left eye became dislodged, and going to Peking, he had operation after operation for four months, to no avail. He was now completely blind, but the help of a Chinese aide allowed him to continue working. Financial pressure on the Canadian mission board caused them to cut the total support for the field to forty-eight dollars per month. Finally, the churches were compelled to go on self-support.

Jonathan was now seventy-five, and he and his wife returned to Canada for furlough. The board scheduled heavy meetings, eight or ten per week. Jonathan began October 1936 with a full schedule of meetings, and on the night of October 7 he gave a long message on the revival in Korea. When Rosalind got up the next morning, the seventy-seven-year-old veteran of the cross was in heaven. During Jonathan's last months, person after person had remarked at how the glory of God seemed to rest upon Jonathan's face as he spoke. Now he was experiencing fully the glory of the Lord's presence.

At Jonathan's funeral at the Knox Presbyterian Church in Toronto, the pastor, Dr. John Inkster, said, "He was a God-intoxicated man—fully surrendered and consecrated. Above all, he was humble. He was baptized with the Holy Ghost and with fire. He was filled with the Spirit because he was emptied of self—therefore he had power which prevailed with God and man. He knew what it was to pray the prayer of faith in the Holy Ghost. He resembled Paul more than he resembled any other man in the Bible."[8]

Madame Guyon————————

*Part 1: Sanctified, Spirit-Filled
Evangel*

Perhaps no writer of the seventeenth century had such a passionate love for Jesus, such a crucified heart, and such victory over the self-life through sanctification by faith as the French mystic known as Madame Guyon.

She was born on April 13, 1648, as Jeanne Marie Bouvières de la Mothe. Her parents were French aristocrats and highly respected, very religious Roman Catholics. Jeanne lived and died a Roman Catholic, untouched by the Reformation, which had begun in Germany a century earlier. God led her in her spiritual pilgrimage to the experience of salvation by faith and later sanctification by faith. She spent years in prison because of her beliefs, but remained true to the Christ she so passionately loved.

Madame Guyon matured in grace through faithfulness in the midst of great sufferings, persecutions, and finally imprisonments. Her holy life greatly influenced many in Europe, and her anointed writings had a profound effect on the Roman Catholic archbishop Fénelon, the Society of Friends, and John Wesley.

Shortly after her birth, Jeanne nearly died of a serious illness. From then on, repeatedly throughout her life, Satan seemed to try to destroy her physically through illness, accidents, and dangers. At the age of two and a half years, she was placed by her parents in an Ursuline convent, and much of her time from then until her marriage was spent in various Roman Catholic institutions. When Jeanne was at home, her mother spent very little time with her and left her in the charge of servants. An older half-sister, who was a nun, showed her special love and taught her about God.

At age four Jeanne longed to be a martyr for Jesus, and the nuns amused themselves by persecuting her, telling her they were going to sacrifice her for Jesus. They even held a sword over her head as she knelt on a cloth. She begged to go home but was soon ill again. When she was nearly seven she was placed in another convent. Jeanne prayed in a little chapel dedicated to the Child Jesus and at times fasted for breakfast and placed her food behind the image of Jesus for him to enjoy.[1]

At nine Jeanne almost died from hemorrhaging. She was moved to another convent, where she was greatly neglected and became very thin. She spent almost all of her time reading a Bible she had found, and she began memorizing much of it.

By the time Jeanne was eleven, she was tall and beautiful for her age. Her mother dressed her in finery, and several suitors asked to marry her in spite of her young age. Her father refused. A cousin en route to be a missionary in China visited her home, and she was greatly impressed. When she could she spent the whole day reading and praying. She wrote the name of Jesus on a piece of paper, and with ribbons and a needle fastened it to her breast, where she kept it for a long time.

A TRAGIC MARRIAGE

In her early teens Jeanne had her spiritual ups and downs. Her family moved to Paris when she was fifteen and plunged into the fashion, culture, and gaiety of the city. Jeanne was tall, beautiful, refined, and a remarkable conversationalist. Her brilliant mind attracted people to her. Many men sought her in marriage, and when she was sixteen her father forced her to marry a thirty-eight-year-old wealthy society man named Jacques Guyon. Jeanne had no choice in the matter and did not even see him until a few days before the wedding.

Jeanne was taken to the home of her mother-in-law, who ruled the house, including Jeanne's husband, like a tyrant. Jeanne was scolded from morning till night, told to be quiet, and kept under her mother-in-law's surveillance. Her new family sneered at her refined ways. Only rarely was she permitted to visit her parents' home. And when she returned from such a visit, she was belittled by her jealous mother-in-law, who tried in every way possible to irritate her.

Jacques and Jeanne altogether had five children.

But soon after their marriage, Jacques became ill. Jeanne was not allowed to wait on him, and a nurse was hired, who sided with the mother-in-law against Jeanne. Jacques never became fully well, and he died twelve years later.

In the midst of this unhappy marriage, a godly Franciscan brother came to Jeanne's area "seeking souls" when she was twenty years old. She talked with him and told of her heart hunger and struggles. God used his words to lead her to an experience of the new birth through faith in Christ on July 22, 1668.

Jeanne's circumstances did not change, but the peace of God flooded her soul. Seeing her transformed life, her society friends ridiculed and persecuted her. Her mother-in-law was more bitter than ever and partly succeeded in turning Jeanne's husband against her. She suffered in silence. She still struggled with pride of heart and the love of attracting others' attention. At some society parties to which she and her husband were invited, she shared too much in their worldly spirit and afterward wept before God. For three months she did not feel God's presence.

Jeanne asked God to take away her pride at any cost. God answered her by letting her contract smallpox. Her mother-in-law left her uncared for even when she was on the verge of death. At last she recovered, but her much praised beauty had been destroyed by the scars of the disease. She rejoiced in this, thinking she could now conquer her pride. At this time God began to help her write religious poetry.

Jeanne's favorite son became ill with smallpox and died. His death was followed by the death of her father and then of a daughter a few days later. The anniversary of Jeanne's new birth was approaching, and a very dear friend, a godly nun, wrote to her suggesting that she observe this spiritual anniversary in a special sacred way, with prayer, alms-giving, and a marriage covenant with Jesus. The nun prepared a form for her to use.

While this consecration contract may seem very strange to us, God used this unusual means to bring Jeanne to experience sanctification by faith. Following is the marriage covenant she copied, signed, and sealed with her ring.

> July 22, 1674
>
> I henceforth take Jesus Christ to be mine. I promise to receive Him as a Husband to me. And I give myself to Him, unworthy though I am, to be His spouse. I ask of Him, in this marriage of spirit with spirit, that I may be of the same mind with Him,—meek, pure, nothing in myself, and united in God's will. And pledge as I am to be His, I accept, as a part of my marriage portion, the temptations and sorrows, the crosses and contempt which fell to Him.
>
> Jeanne M. B. De La Mothe Guyon[2]

About this time a group of men concocted a diabolical scheme to extort a large sum of money from Jacques Guyon. Included in the group was the eldest brother of the king of France and Jeanne's half-brother, Father La Mothe. Her husband so feared a member of the royal family that he refused to contest, but Jeanne, after much prayer, went to the judge on the day of the trial and explained all so clearly that the judge settled the case and exonerated Mr. Guyon.

This greatly pleased Jeanne's husband because it saved him a huge monetary sum. They were very happy together the last few months before he died. She was able to stay by his bedside day and night the last twenty-four days. At age twenty-eight Jeanne was left a widow with three children. She tried to be reconciled with her mother-in-law but without success. So she moved with her children into a small house, and the mother-in-law was never heard from again.

A Deeper Experience

One day, two years after her conversion, as Jeanne was walking with her footman across a bridge in Paris near the cathedral of Notre Dame, a poor monk suddenly joined them and began to talk about spiritual things. He seemed to know about her history, her virtues, and her faults. She said, "He gave me to understand that God required not merely a heart of which it could only be said it is forgiven, but a heart which could properly, and in some real sense, be designated as *holy,* that it was not sufficient to escape hell, but that He demanded also the subjection of the evils of our nature, and the utmost purity and height of Christian attainment."[3]

Jeanne testified, "The Spirit of God bore witness to what he said. The words of this remarkable man, whom I never saw before, and whom I have never seen since, penetrated my very soul." She resolved, "From this day, this hour, if it be possible, I will be wholly the Lord's. The world shall have no portion in me."[4] This was the time when she seems to have entered into the experience of sanctification by faith.

Darkness and Trials

About two years before Jacques died, Jeanne had entered into a six-year period of sorrow, emptiness, darkness, and trial. She lost the awareness of God's presence and had to live by naked faith as she passed through her "dark night of the soul." No religious counselor seemed able to understand her or help her.

After nearly seven years Jeanne felt led to write about her case to a Father La Combe, her brother's friend who had been introduced to her some years before. He explained to her the difference between sorrow and sin. God was removing all earthly props from her but had not forsaken her. She was still unsatisfied. In July 1680 she wrote to Father La Combe, asking him to make July 22, the anniversary of her new birth, a special day of prayer for her. He fasted and prayed that day as she prayed. God answered prayer and lifted the darkness, and she could now live by Galatians 2:20: "I am crucified with Christ: nevertheless I live; yet not I, but Christ liveth in me: and the life which I now live in the flesh I live by the faith of the Son of God, who loved me, and gave himself for me."

One day in a church Jeanne was approached by a priest who said to her, "Do what the Lord has made known to you."

"What else could God require of me, but to take due care of my children?" she asked.

He replied that he didn't know her case, but that she must be willing to leave her children if need be to do God's will.

For the rest of Jeanne's life, her half-brother, Father La Mothe, tried to dominate her and obtain her wealth for his own use. He circulated false stories about her from time to time, charged her with heresy before Roman Catholic officials, and did everything he could to make her come under his power. Jeanne got away from him by slipping away with her six-year-old daughter, a devout woman, and two servants. She had left her sons in the care of a person who would educate them. She departed Paris in July 1681 and began the latter period of her life, which was filled until her death with wanderings, persecutions, imprisonments, and exile.

God Opens Wider Ministry

Jeanne's first stop was a convent in Gex, a French city near the Swiss border. She was unsure of what God wanted her to do but thought perhaps it was to make and apply ointments for the sick and needy. She had no will but to do God's will. She was so absorbed in the peace and joy of her Christian experience that she did not even think of what to call it. Gradually God led her to see that it was sanctification by faith.

God began leading spiritually hungry people to Jeanne, and soon she was counseling people from early morning until late at night. Father La Combe, who had been such a blessing to her, came to visit her. God showed her that he was not sanctified. And she was able, over a period of time, to lead him into the assurance of this wonderful experience of sanctification: inner purity, cleansing, and power, no anger or resentment. From then on, he was her friend and defender when all else turned against her.

La Combe fearlessly preached this "new doctrine" even though Catholic authorities did not believe in salvation by faith, much less sanctification by faith.[5] La Combe was investigated by the church and branded as a heretic. Nevertheless, he fearlessly kept preaching. Then opposition gathered around Jeanne until she had to flee with her daughter and board in another convent. She immersed herself for days in God's Word, much of which she had memorized.

Referring to her new experience, Jeanne wrote, "I was restored, as it were, to perfect life, and set wholly at liberty.... He returned to me with unspeakable magnificence and purity.... I was brought into such harmony with the will of God, that I might now be said to possess not merely consolation, but the God of consolation; not merely peace, but the God of peace."[6]

She added, "As a sanctified heart is always in harmony with the divine providences, I had no will but the divine will." And again: "One characteristic of this higher degree of experience was a sense of inward purity. My mind had such a oneness with God, such a unity with the divine nature, that nothing seemed to have power to spoil it and to diminish its purity."[7]

One writer says:

> Her soul was all ablaze with the unction and power of the Holy Spirit, and everywhere she went she was besieged by multitudes of hungry, thirsty souls, who flocked to her for the spiritual meat that they failed to get from their regular pastors. Revivals of religion began in almost every place visited by her, and all over France earnest Christians began to seek this deeper experience taught by her. Father La Combe began to spread the doctrine with great unction and power. Then the great Archbishop Fénelon was led into a deeper experience through the prayers of Madame Guyon, and he too began to spread the teaching all over France.[8]

Madame Guyon led many to turn their backs on worldliness and sinfulness and to consecrate their lives wholly to God, but worldly priests and Catholic leaders condemned her teaching and refused to walk in the light. They began to persecute Madame Guyon, Father La Combe, Archbishop Fénelon, and all who were teaching this "new doctrine" of "pure love," or "entire death to the self-life."[9]

Madame Guyon

Part 2: Anointed Writer

God used Madame Guyon's pen tremendously. Her spiritual commentaries on the Bible alone filled twenty volumes. Her poems were a great blessing to many and were frequently quoted. She kept a wide correspondence with people, providing counsel and leading them into spiritual victory. Later in Madame Guyon's life Father La Combe insisted that she write her autobiography.

Madame Guyon wrote a tract entitled "A Short Method of Prayer," which a Catholic official saw on her desk, asked to read, and then published. It was distributed widely because there were hungry hearts everywhere. One group of wandering monks bought fifteen hundred copies to distribute. The Roman Catholic Church then branded Madame Guyon a heretic, and she had to flee to Italy. Frail in body, she and her daughter and two faithful maidservants she had led to the Lord were carried in curtained litters over the treacherous mountain paths.

For three months Madame Guyon had refuge with a woman of noble birth in Turin, Italy. Then God led her to return by the same dangerous route to Grenoble, France. She could not remain hidden, and soon, as in previous centers, she was praying with and counseling a stream of hungry souls who came to her door. She used some of her wealth to establish a small hospital. Soon the opposition became so dangerous she had to flee to Marseilles.

The boat in which Madame Guyon was riding was wrecked, but she escaped. After only eight days she was forced to retreat to her friend, the Marchioness of Purnai, in Turin. She went as far as Nice by litter, but the men would carry her no further. She started to go part way to Turin by sea, but a terrible storm turned a one-day trip by boat into a ferocious seven-day storm. Then she started by land but was attacked by a band of robbers.

When the Bishop of Verceil heard that Madame Guyon had arrived in his city, he welcomed her and put her in the home of his niece temporarily, where the Marchioness came to visit her. Madame Guyon again became seriously ill. She was led to return again to Paris, where she was reunited with her nine-year-old daughter and her maid, who had been like a spiritual daughter to her at Grenoble. She finally reached Paris on July 22, 1686, the anniversary of her spiritual birth.

In Paris Madame Guyon rented a home and gathered her three children to her. Her writings were now known all over France. Spiritually thirsty people again came to her, especially many ladies of the nobility. Father La Combe continued to preach the "new doctrine" of sanctification by faith. Madam Guyon's half-brother initiated opposition, and Father La Combe was arrested and imprisoned in the Bastille among other places and spent the next twenty-seven years as a prisoner, until he died.[1]

Within three months of Father La Combe's imprisonment, Madame Guyon's half-brother had her also branded as a heretic, and she was imprisoned for nine months. One of her friends, a close friend of the queen, pled for Madame Guyon, and the king secured her release. She began to counsel ladies of the nobility in Paris and was entertained by the queen often in the palace at Versailles. Her daughter married into a godly family, and she lived with her daughter for two years.

In 1692 Madame Guyon again rented a home in Paris and counseled those seeking spiritual help. And again she was persecuted and was interrogated by bishops and archbishops in an attempt to determine if she was a heretic. During this stressful time she was seriously ill for forty days.[2]

YEARS OF IMPRISONMENT

Madame Guyon was imprisoned in Meaux for six months and then released. On December 27, 1695, she was arrested again, as was her faithful maid, and they were imprisoned in Vincennes.[3] Madame Guyon composed sacred songs, and her maid memorized them. After one year they were moved to a prison in Vaugirard for two years. Madame Guyon's treatment was harsher and harsher. In 1698 she was moved to solitary confinement in a dungeon in the Bastille, where she was held for four years. Her enemies poisoned her in prison, and she suffered the effects of the poison for many years.

Madame Guyon testified, "While I was a prisoner at Vincennes, I passed my time in great peace. I sang songs of joy, which the maid who served me learned by heart, as fast as I made them; and we together sang Thy praises, O my God! The stones of my prison looked like rubies; I esteemed them more than all the gaudy brilliancies of a vain world. My heart was full of that joy which Thou givest them who love Thee, in the midst of their greatest crosses."[4] This is one of the songs she composed:

GOD IS HERE

Strong are walls around me,
    That hold me all the day;
But they who thus have bound me
    Cannot keep God away:
My very dungeon walls are dear
    Because the God I love is here.

They know, who thus oppress me,
    'Tis hard to be alone;

But know not One can bless me
   Who comes through bars and stone.
He makes my dungeon's darkness bright
   And fills my bosom with delight.

In 1702, when Madame Guyon was fifty-four years old, she was set free. She was allowed to visit her daughter, the Countess of Vaux. After a short visit, she was banished to Blois, a hundred miles from Paris, for the rest of her life. There she died on June 9, 1717, at the age of seventy.

SPIRIT-TAUGHT AND ANOINTED IN WRITING

Madame Guyon's communion with Christ was so personal and sweet, and her joy and peace so overflowing, that at times her prison cell seemed like a palace. Many of her poems and books—sixty volumes in all—were written while she was in prison. Some of her poems were translated into English by the poet William Cowper.

She said of her writing:

> I was specially moved to read the Holy Scriptures. When I began I was impelled to write the passage, and instantly its explication was given me, which I also wrote, going on with inconceivable expedition. Before I wrote I knew not what I was going to write. And after I had written, I remembered nothing of what I had penned, nor could I make use of it for the help of souls; but the Lord gave me, at the time I spoke to them, without any reflection, all that was necessary. Thus the Lord made me go on with an explanation of the holy, internal sense of the Scriptures. I had no other book but the Bible. Writing on the Old Testament, I made use of passages of the New without seeking them; they were given me along with the explication; and in writing on the New Testament, and therein making use of the Old, they were given me in like manner. I had scarce any time for writing but in the night, allowing only one or two hours to sleep. The Lord made me write with so much purity that I was obliged to leave off or begin again as He was pleased to order. He proved me every way herein. . . .[5]

I still continued writing with a prodigious swiftness; for the hand could scarcely follow fast enough the Spirit which dictated. The transcriber could not copy in five days what I wrote in one night. Whatever is good in it comes from God only. Whatever is otherwise, from myself. In the day I had scarcely time to eat, by reason of the vast numbers of people which came thronging to me. I wrote the Canticles in a day and a half, and received several visits besides.

A considerable part of the book of Judges was lost. Being desired to render that book complete, I wrote over again the places lost. Afterwards they were found. My former and latter explication were found to be perfectly conformable to each other, which greatly surprised persons of knowledge and merit, who attested to the truth of it.

A counselor of the Parliament, a servant of God, finding on my table a tract on prayer I had written long before, desired me to lend it. He lent it to friends to whom he thought it might be of service. Everyone wanted copies of it. He resolved to have it printed. They requested me to write a preface, and thus was that little book printed which has since made so much noise and been the pretense for several persecutions. This counselor was one of my intimate friends, in a pattern of piety. The book has passed through five editions; and our Lord has given a great benediction to it. Those good friars took fifteen hundred of them.[6]

I was astonished at myself. There was nothing which I was not fit for, or in which I did not succeed. Those who observed this said I had a prodigious capacity. I know I had but meager capabilities, but that in God my spirit had received a quality it never had before. I experienced something of the state the apostles were in after they received the Holy Spirit.[7]

She experienced an almost mystical union of her will with God's will, living out Jesus' desire for his people to be at one with him and the Father (John 17:21).

SATANIC ATTACKS

Satan not only caused Madame Guyon to experience severe accidents, but at times he appeared to her in a frightful vision, shook her bed for as much as fifteen minutes at a time, and broke objects in her room.[8] Nevertheless, she calmly continued her life of prayer and obedience. In spite of careless handling and sometimes deliberate mishandling of her papers and funds by others, God in a series of amazing providence protected them and restored them to her.

THE COMMAND OF FAITH

Madame Guyon was imprisoned a total of ten years and then banished, yet she refused to cease leading others into the wonderful salvation she had in Christ. And at times God honored her faith for healing, and people she prayed for were made well. She would pray a prayer of faith and then by faith command sickness to leave, often with amazing instant results in those who responded in faith.

She too was healed by faith. Once when she was violently sick and convulsing in pain, Father La Combe visited her and expected her to die. Suddenly he felt led to raise his hands and command death to relinquish its hold on her. She was healed instantly.

ANOINTED IN MINISTRY

At times Madame Guyon left herself entirely in God's hands, refusing to plan for herself. God would guide her spiritual friends to tell her the next move to take and would open contacts and ministry to hundreds of people. When widows, maids, worldly men, priests, friars, even bishops came to her, God would give her discernment of their needs and the words to speak to them.

When spies came, pretending to be seekers, God gave Madame Guyon discernment of their true purpose and closed her mouth, and she was unable to speak a word. They left mocking her as a simpleton unable even to speak. Yet as soon as they were gone, God opened her mouth, and she continued counseling and praying with others.

TEACHING PEOPLE TO PRAY

Madame Guyon taught many, including young girls who were hard-working wives beaten by their husbands, to pray in their hearts to God.[9] Priests and friars became so incensed at her that they commanded the people not to pray, saying that prayer was only for the clergy and that they would refuse to absolve the sins of the people unless they stopped praying. Some friars campaigned against Madame Guyon, ordering all her books on prayer to be brought to the town square and publicly burned. The townspeople testified to the changed lives of the praying people and rose up in rebellion until the bishop had to insist that the friars had gone too far.

In the meantime God brought other friars to Madame Guyon, and she was able to lead them to Christ. Even superior officials in the same Catholic brotherhood as the friars were totally transformed. One chief official who had been a friar for forty years said that Madame Guyon's book had taught him how to pray.[10] On one occasion she listed among her recent "children" in Christ "a great number of nuns, virtuous young women, men of the world, priests, friars, three curates, one canon, and one grand-vicar." She could have added several more bishops and an archbishop.

A LIFE OF CONTENTMENT

Madame Guyon wrote a poem she called "A Little Bird I Am" while she was imprisoned in the dungeon of the Bastille that expresses her contentment in life no matter what her situation. It reads:

> A little bird I am,
> Shut in from fields of air,
> And in my cage I sit and sing,
> To him who placed me there;
> Well pleased a prisoner to be,
> Because, my God, it pleases thee!
>
> Naught have I else to do,
> I sing the whole day long;
> And he whom I most love to please
> Doth listen to my song;
> He caught and bound my wandering wing,
> And still he bends to hear me sing.

Thou hast an ear to hear,
    A heart to love and bless;
And though my notes were e'er so rude,
    Thou wouldst not hear the less;
Because thou knowest as they fall,
    That love, sweet love, inspires them all.

My cage confines me round,
    Abroad I cannot fly;
But though my wing is closely bound,
    My heart's at liberty;
My prison walls cannot control
    The flight, the freedom of the soul.

Oh, it is good to soar,
    These bolts and bars above,
To him whose purpose I adore,
    Whose providence I love;
And in thy mighty will to find
    The joy, the freedom of the mind.[11]

In spite of her repeated sufferings and years of imprisonment and in spite of seldom being able to pray with others who shared her doctrine or commitment, Madame Guyon, Jeanne Marie Bouvières de la Mothe, became one of the greatest Christian leaders of all time. Her life story, her hymns, and her books have influenced thousands for three centuries.

Frances Ridley Havergal

Spirit-filled Singer and Writer

Frances Ridley Havergal was born December 14, 1836, of godly English parents. Her father was a minister of the Church of England and was an accomplished composer and musician. She was the youngest of six children, a beautiful, vivacious child with golden curls, the pet of the family. She loved to romp and climb trees and was always active.

PRECOCIOUS AS A CHILD

Frances was precocious mentally and spiritually. She loved to sit on her father's knee as he read the Bible and loved to sing Christian songs. The happy home was blessed by the prayers, cheerful ways, godly example, and love of both parents.

At age three Frances was reading simple books. At four she was fluent in reading the Bible and in writing. By age seven she was writing poetry. She also began studying languages at an early age and in time became proficient in German, French, Greek, Hebrew, Italian, Latin, and Welsh.

Frances was deeply convicted by a sermon when she was six years old but did not tell anyone about it for two years. Instead, she took refuge in God's Word and in prayer. At age eight she spoke to a minister about her spiritual need, but he did not lead her to the Lord. He told her to be a good child and pray. For five more years she lived under conviction of sin, loving the Lord but lacking the assurance of salvation. During this time, when Frances was twelve, her mother died. Her mother's dying instructions to her were: "Pray God to prepare you for all He is preparing for you."

Before Frances's fourteenth birthday she was placed in a girls' boarding school in England that was directed by a godly woman. A revival broke out in the school, and many of the girls were born again and became so happy "their faces shone with a heavenly radiance."[1] Frances felt more deeply convicted of her sin than ever yet did not receive assurance of forgiveness, although she prayed very earnestly. One day Frances confided in a friend, Caroline Cooke, who later became her stepmother. Miss Cooke urged Frances to trust herself to Jesus at once. Frances left her suddenly, ran upstairs, and fell on her knees. At last she had the secret. She trusted Jesus completely and was filled with assurance and joy. "Earth and heaven seemed bright from that moment—I did trust the Lord Jesus," she wrote.[2]

From that time on Frances was a bold witness for Jesus wherever she went. When she attended a private boarding school in Germany, she was the only born-again girl there, and she endured persecution from the "worldly" girls. She witnessed and prayed in a one-girl campaign for their salvation. By the time she was seventeen she had completed her education.

By age twenty-two Frances had memorized all of the Gospels, Epistles, Revelation, Psalms, and Isaiah. Later she memorized the Minor Prophets.

POET, SINGER, AND MUSICIAN

Frances asked the Lord to guide and anoint her in her writing, to give her every word, even the rhyming in her poetry. God anointed her again and again. Her sweet spirit was obvious to people, and the deep spiritual tone of all she wrote gave her a ministry in great demand. She sent some of her poems to Christian magazines, and her father composed music for some of them. Frances also composed music herself. She was an unusually gifted pianist and played the music of Handel, Beethoven, and Mendelssohn without reading the music. A contralto soloist, she sang in the Philharmonic concerts of the day to the appreciation and applause of the crowds, yet she was committed to singing only sacred songs she could sing to the glory of God.

At age twenty-one, as Frances stood in an art gallery at Dusseldorf, Germany, gazing at the famous painting of Christ by Albrecht Dürer, *Ecce Homo* (Behold the Man), she was so deeply moved by love for Christ that she wrote the beloved hymn:

> I gave My life for thee,
>   My precious blood I shed,
> That thou might ransomed be,
>   And quickened from the dead;
> I gave, I gave My life for thee,
>   What hast thou giv'n me?
>
> I suffered much for thee,
>   More than thy tongue can tell,
> Of bitterest agony,
>   To rescue thee from hell;
> I've borne, I've borne it all for thee,
>   What hast thou borne for Me?

CONSTANT WITNESS

Frances seized every opportunity for witness. One morning in the Alps she found a quiet spot by a mountain stream and began to write a poem about God, but she told the Lord she was willing if he had anything else for her to do. She had written the first four lines of her poem when a farm laborer stopped beside her to get a drink from the stream. She started to speak to him about the Water of Life. Within minutes the man's two sons came through the bushes and sat down beside their father, listening to her share the gospel. When the three left, she started on her poem again but had only written one or two lines when one of the boys returned, this time with his sister, so she too could hear the gospel.

FILLED WITH THE SPIRIT

For years Frances longed for a deeper, fuller, richer Christian experience. She prayed and longed to be truly filled with the Spirit. She wrote in 1865, "Oh, that He may make me a vessel sanctified and meet for the Master's use!"[3] Wherever she went she longed for the deeper experience she saw pictured in God's Word.

Her sister Maria describes how Frances finally received the full cleansing and empowering of the Spirit-filled life. Late in 1873, when Frances was thirty-seven, someone sent her a tiny volume entitled *All for Jesus*. It described the full spiritual experience for which she longed. Wrote Maria:

> She was gratefully conscious of having for many years loved the Lord and delighted in His service; but there was in her experience a falling short of the standard, not so much of a holy walk and conversation, as of uniform brightness and continuous enjoyment in the divine life. *All for Jesus,* she found, went straight to the point of the need and longing of her soul. Writing in reply to the author of the book, she said, "I do so long for deeper and fuller teaching in my own heart. *All for Jesus* has touched me very much. . . . I know I love Jesus and there are times when I feel such intensity of love for Him that I have not words to describe it. I rejoice too in Him as my 'Master' and 'Sovereign,' but I want to come nearer still, to have the full realization of John 14:21 and to know 'the power of His resurrection,' even if it be with the fellowship of His sufferings. And all this, not exactly for my own joy alone, but for others. . . . So I want Jesus to speak to me, to say 'many things' to me, that I may speak for Him to others with real power. It is not knowing doctrine, but *being with* Him, which will give this."[4]

One of Frances's famous hymns emphasizes her sentiments:

Lord, speak to me, that I may speak
    In living echoes of Thy tone;

As Thou hast sought, so let me seek
　　Thy erring children lost and lone.

O use me, Lord, use even me,
　　Just as Thou wilt and when and where;
Until Thy blessed face I see,
　　Thy rest, Thy joy, Thy glory share.

Frances knew God had been leading her thus far. Now, on December 2, 1873, she was pointed to God's promise in 1 John 1:7, "The blood of Jesus Christ his Son cleanseth us from all sin." "I see it all, and I have the blessing," she joyously testified.[5] In Frances's own words, this new experience had instantly "lifted her whole life into sunshine, of which all she had previously experienced was but as pale and passing April gleams compared with the fullness of summer glory."[6]

Maria wrote, "The practical effect of this was most evident in her daily true-hearted, whole-hearted, service for her King, and also in the increased joyousness of the unswerving obedience of her home life, the surest test of all."[7]

So Frances wrote her hymn, which began:

I am trusting Thee, Lord Jesus,
　　Trusting only Thee;
Trusting Thee for full salvation,
　　Great and free.

Frances expounded on the meaning of the song:

Have we not been limiting 1 John 1:7, by practically making it refer only to "remission of sins that are past" instead of taking the grand simplicity of "cleanseth us from *all* sin?" "All" is *all;* and as we may trust Him to cleanse us from the stain of past sins, so we may trust Him to cleanse us from all present defilement; yes, all! If not, we take away from this most precious promise, and by refusing to take it in its fullness lose the fullness of its application and power. Then we limit God's power to keep; we look at our frailty more than

His omnipotence.... It was that one word *"cleanseth"* which opened the door of a very glory of hope and joy to me. I had never seen the force of the tense before, a continual present, always a present tense, not a present which the next moment becomes a past. It *goes on* cleansing, and I have no words to tell how my heart rejoices in it. Not a coming to be cleansed in the fountain only, but a remaining in the fountain, so that it may and can go on cleansing.[8]

Why should we pare down the promises of God to the level of what we have hitherto experienced, of what God is "able to do," or even of what we have thought He might be able to do for us? Why not receive God's promises, nothing doubting, just as they stand?[9]

Frances wrote to Maria:

One arrives at the same thing starting almost from anywhere. Take Philippians 4:19, "Your need"; well, what is my great need and craving of soul? Surely it is now, (having been justified by faith, and having assurance of salvation,) to be made holy by the continual sanctifying power of God's Spirit; to be kept from grieving the Lord Jesus; to be kept from thinking or doing whatever is not accordant with His holy will. Oh *what* a need is this! And it is said "He *shall* supply all your need"; now, shall we turn around and say "all" does not mean quite all? Both as to the commands and promises, it seems to me that everything short of believing them *as they stand* is but another form of "yea hath God said?"...One of the intensest moments of my life was when I saw the force of that word *"cleanseth,"* the utter unexpected and altogether unimagined sense of its fulfillment to me, on simply believing it in its fullness, was just indescribable. I experienced nothing like it short of heaven.[10]

THE HYMN WRITER

Frances's few remaining years were the most blessed and most fruitful of her life. Her best hymns were written after this powerful spiritual experience. Shortly afterward she wrote her great consecration hymn, "Take My Life." She wrote:

Perhaps you will be interested to know the origin of the consecration hymn, "Take My Life." I went for a little visit of
five days. There were ten persons in the house, some uncon-
verted and long prayed for, some converted but not rejoicing Christians. He gave me the prayer, "Lord, give me *all* in
this house!" And He just *did!* Before I left the house everyone had got a blessing. The last night of my visit I was too
happy to sleep and passed most of the night in praise and
renewal of my consecration, and these little couplets formed
themselves and chimed in my heart one after another, till they
finished with, *"Ever, only, 'ALL for Thee'!"*[11]

Take my life and let it be
    Consecrated, Lord, to Thee;
Take my hands and let them move
    At the impulse of Thy love,
    At the impulse of Thy love.

Take my feet and let them be
    Swift and beautiful for Thee;
Take my voice and let me sing
    Always, only, for my King,
    Always, only, for my King.

Take my lips and let them be
    Filled with messages for Thee;
Take my silver and my gold,
    Not a mite would I withhold,
    Not a mite would I withhold.

Take my love, my God, I pour
    At Thy feet its treasure store;
Take myself and I will be
    Ever, only, all for Thee,
    Ever, only, all for Thee.

Frances used all of her talents for the Lord, teaching Sunday
school; conducting church choirs; speaking in tent meetings; wit-

nessing at meetings in the homes of the wealthy, to tourists and villagers in vacation spots in the mountains, and to working girls in the laundry; leading the YWCA Prayer Union, and lecturing on hymnology in fashionable girls' schools. Whether she spoke in English, French, or German, her theme was always the same.

Proceeds from the publishing of Frances's poems, hymns, and books were generously given to support God's work at home or on the mission field. She wrote:

> The Lord has shown me another little step, and of course I have taken it with extreme delight. "Take my silver and my gold," now means shipping off all ornaments (including the jewel cabinet which is really fit for a Countess) to the Church Missionary House, where they will be disposed of for me. I had no idea I had such a jeweler's shop, nearly fifty articles being packed off. I don't think I need tell you I never packed a box with such pleasure.[12]

Frances had given all her jewelry for missions.

During a bout with typhoid fever, Frances wrote the hymn "Like a River Glorious," which describes her Spirit-filled life. She seemed more frail in her last years, but in between periods of illness and physical collapse she went out singing, evangelizing, lecturing, and working for Jesus. The longer she continued in the Spirit-filled life, the more glorious and precious the fullness of the Spirit became.

> Like a river glorious
>   Is God's perfect peace,
> Over all victorious
>   In its bright increase;
> Perfect, yet it floweth
>   Fuller every day,
> Perfect, yet it groweth
>   Deeper all the way.
>
> Hidden in the hollow
>   Of His blessed hand,

Never foe can follow,
    Never traitor stand;
Not a surge of worry,
    Not a shade of care,
Not a blast of hurry
    Touch the spirit there.

Every joy or trial
    Falleth from above,
Traced upon our dial
    By the Sun of Love.
We may trust Him fully
    All for us to do;
They who trust Him wholly
    Find Him wholly true.

Chorus:
Stayed upon Jehovah,
    Hearts are fully blest;
Finding, as He promised,
    Perfect peace and rest.

Frances wrote to her sister in 1875, "It's no mistake, Maria, about the blessing God sent me December 2, 1873; it is far more distinct than my conversion, I can't date that. I am always happy, and it is *such peace*."[13]

MEETING JESUS FACE TO FACE

One day in May 1879, Frances was holding an outdoor temperance meeting. A sudden cold wind chilled her to the bone. She quickly succumbed to fever, chills, and peritonitis. When her friends expressed their sympathy, she exclaimed, "Never mind! It's home the faster! God's will is delicious. He makes no mistakes." She asked that her favorite text be placed on her tombstone, "The blood of Jesus Christ his Son cleanseth us from all sin."

At the end, the doctor and Frances's family were at her bedside. She asked them to sing some of her hymns. She said, "Ever since I trusted Jesus altogether, I have been so happy. I cannot tell how lovely, how precious He is to me."

The doctor said to her, "You are seriously ill, and the inflammation is increasing."

Frances replied, "I thought so, but if I'm going, it is too good to be true."

Then the doctor said, "Good-bye; I shall not see you again."

"Then do you really think I'm going?" she asked.

"Yes," the doctor answered.

"Today?"

"Probably."

"Beautiful!" Frances exclaimed. "Too good to be true. Splendid to be so near the gates of heaven!"

Suddenly she seemed convulsed with her sickness. "It ceased; the nurse gently assisting her, she nestled down in the pillows, folded her hands on her breast, saying, 'There; now it is all over! Blessed rest!' And now she looked up steadfastly, as if she saw the Lord, and surely, nothing less heavenly could have reflected such a glorious radiance upon her face. For ten minutes we watched that almost visible meeting with her King, and her countenance was so glad, as if she were already talking to Him. Then she tried to sing, but her voice failed; and as her brother commended her soul into her Redeemer's hand, she passed away."[14]

"Ever only, all for Thee" was Frances Ridley Havergal's theme both in life and in death.

John Hyde

Intercessor with a Shining Face

John Hyde is best known as Praying Hyde, "the apostle of prayer" and "the missionary who never sleeps." His father, Dr. Smith Hyde, was a very spiritual Presbyterian minister, who for seventeen years pastored in Carthage, Illinois. Mrs. Hyde, mother of six children, was a beautiful Christian. John was born on November 9, 1865. Over and over Dr. Hyde, at the family altar or in his pulpit, prayed for God to send laborers into his harvest field. God heard those requests, and three of Smith Hyde's own children entered Christian service.

At McCormick Theological Seminary during his senior year, John heard the call to be a missionary, and his soul was set aflame. He talked about missions, prayed about missions, and personally challenged his classmates for missions. One by one he would take them for long walks, pleading God's need of laborers. At graduation in 1892, twenty-six of the forty-six seniors had pledged themselves to be missionaries.

On October 15, 1892, John and five other Presbyterian missionaries sailed for India. When he got to his cabin he found a letter from a minister friend of his father who loved John greatly. Opening the farewell letter, John read, "I shall not cease praying for you, dear John, until you are filled with the Spirit." John was instantly insulted, and his pride was hurt. "I felt exceedingly angry, crushed the letter, threw it into a corner of the cabin and went up on deck in a very angry spirit. The idea of implying that I was *not* filled with the Spirit!"[1]

Angrily, John paced up and down the deck. He knew the holy life of the writer. The man loved him dearly, and John loved him. Down in his heart John felt the writer was correct. He was not really suited to be a missionary. He went back to the cabin, fell on his knees, found the crushed letter, and read it again and again.

INTO THE FULLNESS OF THE SPIRIT

After days of struggle and prayer, John determined that whatever the cost, he would be filled with the Spirit. He had determined to be an outstanding missionary with a mastery of the language. Now he told the Lord he would be willing to fail his language exams, be a missionary working quietly and unnoticed, if only he could be filled with the Spirit.

Although John became more fully consecrated, he still did not have the victory he sought. He attended a street meeting in India one day, where the missionary who was speaking told how Christ was the Savior from sin. At the close of the meeting a man came up and asked the speaker if Christ had actually saved him from all sin. John knew that if he had been asked that question, to be honest, he would have had to say no. There was one besetting sin in John's life. He went to his room and prayed, "Either You must save me from my besetting sin or I must return to America and do other work."[2] He knew he could not honestly preach a victory over sin he did not himself have.

As John prayed, God brought 1 John 1:9 to his heart. He knew he had confessed. He knew God was faithful, and that moment, by faith, he claimed the cleansing Paul in 1 Thessalonians 5:23 terms "through and through." Instantly, God witnessed in his heart that he was able to do it and that he had planned a work for John in India. "He did deliver me, and I have not had a doubt of that since.

I can now stand up without hesitation and testify that He has given me victory and I love to witness to this."[3]

John's friend, Reverend Pengwern Jones, said that when John testified to him of thus being cleansed and filled with the Spirit, his face shown with God's glory. "Can I ever forget his face as he told me these things?"[4] Again and again over the succeeding years, God's glory was seen on the face of Praying Hyde, for from that time on the Spirit's power was on him in a new way.

VILLAGE MINISTRY

John's first years in India were not remarkable. By faithful plodding he became a good speaker of both Urdu and Punjabi. He served as a village missionary, going from village to village on foot or by horse-pulled cart with his Indian coworkers. He took his little tent with him wherever he went.

Being unmarried, John never had a home of his own but stayed in the home of other missionaries when he was not on trek in the villages, or else he lived in his tent. His dying request was to raise funds for missionaries such as himself so that they could have permanent homes of their own. During his nineteen years in India, however, he was completely at home in his small tent, and prayer made it the anteroom of heaven.

John was a slow, quiet speaker and was somewhat hard of hearing. He gave so much time to Bible study that his language progress was slow. When the missionary committee reproved him and threatened to send him back to the United States, he replied, "I must put first things first." He felt that perhaps his deafness would hinder him, so he offered his resignation to the synod. But when the villagers of his area heard of this, they petitioned the synod not to accept his resignation, saying, "If he never speaks the language of our lips, he speaks the language of our hearts."[5]

PRAYER BURDEN FOR REVIVAL

During John's third year in India, God gave him a prayer burden for revival. From then on for some ten years he kept faithfully interceding for revival before God's answer came. The area in which he labored was almost barren, and he saw minimal results.

At times John experienced opposition from non-Christians who did not want the gospel preached to the poor and low-caste people. They stole from him, tried to prevent water carriers from bringing him the water he needed, and threatened to pull down his tent. But John kept itinerating in the villages, staying days or sometimes several weeks in one area and then moving on to another.

John became convinced that just as Jacob wrestled with God for his family, so what India needed if there was to be a breakthrough and spiritual harvest was a wrestling Jacob. "I determined to ask God to give me one real Israel, a wrestler with God, a prince prevailing." While praying with his friend Paterson, John felt that God granted him the power to play the role of a prevailing Israel. Yet he felt inadequate for his new role. "How little I know of the love and power of our Savior. . . . There is mighty power in prayer, but how little I know about it and how feeble is my boldness in approaching Him." Yet so sure was John Hyde of God's will to him to be an Israel for India that he said, "My heart feels joyful and at rest about it all. I know but one word—*obedience*," he wrote.[6]

John loved the Indian people and lived among them, often eating with them and helping them in times of trouble. He was always patient with them—interceding for the non-Christians, people who fell into sin, Christians who lapsed into idolatry, and quarreling Christians. He would gather these people around him, not scolding them, but saying, "Let's pray." Then he would go to his knees, sometimes praying for two or three hours before he arose.

By 1897 John was beginning to see some encouragement in his ministry. In 1898 he wrote, "Our whole mission unites in prayer every Sunday for the outpouring of the Holy Spirit upon us."[7] In 1899 John, though weak in body, began spending whole nights in prayer. He wrote, "Results I have not seen, or but little. . . . I have felt led to pray for others this year as never before. I never before knew what it was to work all day and then pray all night before God for another."[8] Though results were few, he knew God's day of harvest would eventually come, and he was glad to sacrifice time and self.

In 1901 John wrote, "I believe it is to be a time of Pentecostal power, or even a double portion of the Pentecostal spirit. I interpret God as laying a burden of prayer on souls, pouring out the spirit of grace and supplication."[9] So he urged his homeland friends to awaken to the power of prayer. More and more he cried to God to send revival.

After ten years in India, John went on furlough in 1902. Wherever he spoke his main concern was to teach the necessity of the fullness of the Spirit, and he pled for prayer for India. He returned to India with renewed vision.

THE PUNJAB PRAYER UNION

Early in 1904 a spirit of revival descended on a Presbyterian girls' school. From there it spread to the nearby Presbyterian Theological Seminary. Dr. W. B. Anderson sent out a call for prayer warriors to gather in April to intercede for India. John Hyde, R. McCheyne Paterson, and a small group of others gathered for intercession. All were moved by John's prayer habits. They formed the Punjab Prayer Union, named for the province where John was laboring. Those who joined agreed to pray for revival and for more of the Holy Spirit's power in their own lives and work, to set apart a half hour for intercession daily as soon after noon as possible, and to commit themselves to pray for this spiritual awakening until it came.

The Prayer Union then sent out a call for all Christian workers to assemble at Sialkot for a Christian life convention in late August. John and Paterson began thirty days of intercession before the convention to prepare the way of the Lord. After nine days they were joined by a friend and prayer partner, George Turner. For thirty days and nights they agreed in prayer for God's Spirit to be outpoured.

THE SIALKOT CONVENTION

When the convention began two prayer rooms were opened—one for women and one for men. From the first day on neither room was ever vacant. John remained there much of the time. Many Indians also spent hours in the prayer room.

John addressed the convention on the fullness of the Holy Spirit, and as he spoke God revealed to him more deeply than ever before his plan for sanctification by faith. Then John felt they must have more public testimony. He was asked to lead a men's prayer meeting the next night. He felt compelled to confess to the men how he had had tremendous struggles with sin in the past in his own life and how God had given him complete victory. After about fifteen minutes he said, "Let us pray." All fell on their faces before God in Indian fashion. One by one men began to get up and confess to sins and then pray for victory. The meeting went on for hours. Revival had begun.

The 1905 Sialkot convention saw even more of the power of God at work. John, the principal speaker, spoke on the power of the Spirit and the role of the Spirit as the chief witness. "Is the Holy Spirit first in your pulpits?" he asked the pastors. In one service he joyously entered the hall and said three words in Urdu and then in English, repeating it three times, "O Heavenly Father." Suddenly it was as if an ocean tide of the Spirit swept across the group, "a sound from heaven as of a mighty rushing wind."[10] God's love was poured out. Confessions of sins, tears, and songs and shouts of joy abounded as people found spiritual victory. Prayer continued day and night the whole ten days.

THE WEEPING CONVENTION

At the 1906 convention God revealed through John how Christ lives today to intercede and wants us to share his burden for the world. Over and over John would begin to weep over the sins of India and the world. The vision of souls going to hell without Christ broke the hearts of Indians and missionaries. At times the whole assembly wept as they interceded for the lost in the all-night meeting.

Prayer travail continued at the 1907 convention and was interspersed with holy joy and praise to God. John's last message to the convention was on the prayer burden of Paul in Romans 9:1–3, where he said he could wish himself accursed for the sake of his people. The whole assembly was moved to tears with the burden for India.

During 1908 John frequently agonized in prayer and fasting for the non-Christians of the Punjab and of all India. His concern for the salvation of souls was so intense that he lost all hunger for food and slept very little. Nevertheless, he was cheerful around others and children were attracted to him. He always had time to speak and pray with people. The light on his face told of the heavenly communion he was sharing.[11]

ONE, TWO, AND FOUR SOULS PER DAY

During the 1908 convention, in spite of the meager spiritual results the previous years, God led him after hours of intercession to claim by faith one soul per day during the coming year. It meant days of fasting and nights of prayer. But by the end of the year God had helped him to see more than four hundred non-Christians won to Christ and baptized.

In the 1909 convention God used John more mightily than ever before. John emphasized the need for Gethsemane and Calvary love and Gethsemane intercession. He said that Christians needed to have not their own broken hearts, but God's broken heart revealed in them. If self is crucified, dead, and buried with Christ, then the new man will be revived, raised, and seated with Christ in heavenly intercession, sharing Christ's throne (Eph. 2:6). At that convention John agonized and prayed for days until he received God's promise of two souls per day. When the next annual convention convened, more than eight hundred non-Christians had been won to Christ and baptized.[12]

Before the 1910 Sialkot convention John prayed for some weeks until he had the assurance that the next year God would give him four souls per day. God used him all over India in revival and conferences in many of the large cities. He also kept touring his own district. He spent many nights in prayer before the 1910 convention asking for God's power to be present. When he addressed the convention he spoke with tremendous fire and force, and people noted that his face seemed almost transfigured with God's glory.

That year God did give John four souls per day. John had "prayed through" for them. On some days when fewer than four found the Lord, he would be greatly concerned at night and would search his heart. He said that almost inevitably he found that he had not praised the Lord enough, and then when he would catch up with his praising, the Lord would quickly make up the lacking number of souls.

That year John learned to pray about his village trips even more specifically. Often he was led to pray and claim by faith a specific number of souls for a given day. Again and again God gave him that exact number. On more than one occasion the number God promised was ten.

FAREWELL TO INDIA

Always weak in body, by 1911 John became seriously ill. A Calcutta doctor examined him and found his heart had completely moved from his left side to his right side. On March 11 his Indian services ended as he sailed for Britain and home.

While in Wales at the home of his friend, Pengwern Jones, who was on furlough, he heard of Dr. J. Wilbur Chapman's preaching mission at Shrewsbury. Chapman, former coworker of D. L. Moody, for fifty years held evangelistic campaigns across the world and was the first director of the Winona Lake Bible Conference in Indiana.

Chapman was finding little interest in his preaching mission, and many local ministers did not wholeheartedly cooperate. Attendance was very poor. Chapman was told that an American missionary known as Praying Hyde had come to pray down blessing on his ministry. Almost instantly, Chapman said, the tide turned. That night the hall was packed and fifty men surrendered to Jesus Christ when the invitation was given. As they were leaving the building, Chapman turned to John and said, "Mr. Hyde, I want you to pray for me." He took John to his room. Chapman gives the account.

> He came to my room, turned the key in the door, dropped on his knees, waited five minutes without a single syllable coming from his lips. I could hear my own heart thumping and

his beating. I felt the hot tears running down my face. I knew I was with God. Then with upturned face, down which tears streamed, he said, "Oh, God!" Then for five minutes at least he was still again, and then when he knew that he was talking to God, his arm went round my shoulder, and then came up from the depth of his heart such petitions for men as I have never heard before, and I rose from my knees to know what *real* prayer was. We have gone round the world and back again, believing that prayer is mighty, and we believe it as never before.[13]

John remained with Chapman for one week, prevailing in prayer for the services. Then he went back to the home of his friend, Jones. He was so weak he could hardly speak. As Jones leaned over him, he whispered, "The burden was very heavy, but my dear Savior's burden for me took Him down to the grave."[14] John sailed for America, arriving in New York on August 8, 1911. Physicians examined him and advised a brain tumor operation. The tumor was found to be malignant. He went to his sister's home in Massachusetts, and the malignancy spread to his back and side. Despite his weakened condition, he continued to intercede for the lost.

On February 17, 1912, while suffering intense pain, that radiant glow of God's glory that had again and again been seen on his face, lighted up his face once more, and his lips called out, *"Bol! Yisu Masih, Ki Jai!"* That is, "Shout victory to Jesus!" was his dying cry, and he was in heaven with his Great High Priest, the One he had loved above all else, to whom he had committed himself early in life. His body was buried on February 20 in Moss Ridge Cemetery, Carthage, Illinois, beside his father and mother.

EVALUATIONS OF HYDE'S LIFE

John's close friend and biographer, Francis A. McGaw, said the one outstanding characteristic of the life of Praying Hyde was holiness manifested in Christlikeness. John's close friend and biographer, J. Pengwern Jones, said John had three outstanding characteristics: ardent love for Jesus, passionate love for the Indian people among whom he worked, and loving affection for his fellow missionaries.

A Personal Soul Winner

Praying Hyde became known as one of the most effective personal soul winners India ever knew, especially in his latter years. Wherever he went he led souls to Christ. He would stop to speak to a stranger, and soon his hand would be on the stranger's shoulder and he would be praying with that person, leading him to Christ.

When John traveled on the crowded Indian trains, he was always trying to lead another person to Christ. Often by the time he reached his destination he was dealing very directly with another traveler about his salvation but had not yet won him. John would ignore the fact that he was at his destination and would travel further on the train, witnessing and praying. When he had led the person to Christ, if possible he would baptize him and then return by a later train to his own destination. On one occasion he rode past his stopping place four times in order to win the person to whom he was witnessing. When he finally arrived at his destination, having passed through the station four times already, he found that the engagement he was going to attend was over, but heaven was richer with four new believers he had led to Christ en route.

The Ministry of Tears

Praying Hyde's ministry was anointed with tears. He was often seen weeping during private prayer as he interceded for souls. And at times he broke down while praying publicly. As he described the love of Jesus, especially his agony in Gethsemane and Calvary, he would speak with many tears. He believed that Jesus, as he intercedes at the right hand of the Father, prays with great agony for the sins and sinners of our world. This would break John's heart as he shared Christ's burden.

The Ministry of Giving

John was constantly giving away his clothes to persons in need. Often at the Sialkot convention, which had up to two thousand in attendance, he would find someone without a blanket and give his own blanket to that person. And time and again he would take off his coat to give to a needy person.

In one village John won a number of men to the Lord, but their wives refused to respond. He awoke with a tremendous headache one morning, and because his custom was to thank God for everything, he thanked God for his headache. He hungered so to win souls that he asked that he be carried on his bed and put under the shade of a tree beside the road. When the village women learned how ill he was, one by one they came to his bedside to sympathize, and he used their visits as an opportunity to witness. That day he led many of them to the Lord, and that night he had a baptismal service in which he baptized several of them. Then John knew the reason for his severe headache that morning.

The Ministry of Healing

At times in those years, bubonic plague spread from village to village. When John heard how Christians were dying, he went out among them to pray for them, and many were healed. "Jesus is living and can bring and remove pestilence. Have we laid hold of Him and found deliverance from sin's plague?" he asked.[15]

The Man with the Bible

Praying Hyde loved God's Word. From the time he arrived in India, he felt it absolutely essential that he really know the Bible. Over the years his love for the Word became deeper and deeper. Throughout the day, from his first cup of tea in the early morning, whenever possible his Bible was in his hand. When he witnessed to people, when he prayed with people, the Bible was always in his hand or close beside him. Usually when he knelt to pray in his tent, in his room, or in a prayer room, the Bible lay open before him. Often his hands rested on it as he claimed the promises of God and grounded his whole praying upon them. The Bible was his constant strength.

THE JOY OF THE LORD

Another source of repeated renewal of strength was his joy in the Lord. In the midst of tremendous wrestling in prayer he would often break out into songs of joy. Sometimes in prayer he would be so thrilled by the presence and promises of God and so filled with faith that he would break out into holy laughter. He was very much at home with the Indian custom of praising the Lord by calling *"Bol! Yisu Masih, Ki Jai!"*—"Shout victory to Jesus!"

During revival times at Sialkot, when John led someone to victory in the prayer room, he would stand up, smile, and begin to sing, " 'Tis done, the great transaction's done" (from the hymn "O Happy Day!"). Often he became so full of joy that he would clap his hands or even leap for joy. At times such blessing was poured out that the whole convention group not only rose to their feet and sang and shouted, *"Bol! Yisu Masih, Ki Jai!"* but would do a hallelujah march around the room as well. His close friends recall that often in the middle of the night he would get so blessed he would sing praises to God. This always renewed his strength.

John Hyde expressed the hope that other people would not try to duplicate his life. He knew his was a special call from God, and he was faithful unto death. Our responsibility is to be faithful to God's call for our lives. God needs only one John Hyde, but he needs many others to become mighty intercessors in the service of Christ, following God as faithfully in their calling as John Hyde did in his.

10

Adoniram Judson ——————

Part 1: God's Apostle to Burma

Adoniram Judson was born August 9, 1788, in the home of a Congregational minister who had ambitions for his son to become great. Adoniram enrolled in a small Rhode Island college, which later became Brown University. While there, he became a close friend of another student who put skeptical thoughts into his mind, and Adoniram became a deist. He graduated as valedictorian.

After graduation, Adoniram shocked his parents when they discovered he was a deist. His father argued and his mother prayed. One day while traveling by horseback Adoniram came to a village, where he spent the night in an inn. The inn had only one empty room that night, and it was next to a room where he was told a young man was critically ill, perhaps dying. Adoniram wondered if the sick young man was ready to die. Then he began to think about death. His thoughts terrified him, yet he wondered what his skeptic friend would think if he knew he had such thoughts.

In the morning Adoniram dressed quickly, and after breakfast as he left he asked whether the young man in the adjoining room was better. He was told no, he had died. Judson asked who he was. To his amazement, it was his skeptic friend who had led him into deism. Adoniram was stunned, and over and over in his mind came the words, "Lost! Lost!" All his parents had taught him came back to him. God in his providence had arranged for him to be in the room next to his friend who had died without God. He suddenly realized the Bible was true and the God of the Bible was real.

When Adoniram returned home two visitors came to his father's home who discussed a new seminary in which they would be professors. They were immediately impressed with Adoniram, but they knew he needed time to get over his deistic thinking. He enrolled as a special student, not as a ministerial student, in Andover Theological College.

CONVERSION AND CALL

In a few weeks Adoniram began to see the weakness of skepticism and dedicated himself to God. His heart was at peace. His doubts were gone. The next summer he joined his father's church.

The following year Adoniram read a missionary sermon on India. God touched his heart, but there was no American missionary society and no American missionary in the world. He thought Bible translation work would be needed and his Hebrew and Greek studies would help him. He talked enthusiastically with people but was ridiculed.

One snowy day as he walked along through the woods God spoke to him from Mark 16:15, "Go ye into all the world, and preach the gospel to every creature." From that moment he never doubted God's will for his life. He was offered the position of assistant pastor at the largest church in Boston. Adoniram was horrified. He told his family that he was called to Burma, about which he had been reading. His mother and sister wept day after day. His father was silent. Adoniram expected even worse at Andover. Instead, he found four students to whom God had spoken about missions yet didn't know where God would have them go. Adoniram persuaded them of the need of Asia. Eventually there were seven in all.

At the Congregational General Association of the Commonwealth on June 28, 1810, Adoniram presented a petition he had carefully prepared and had signed by four of the students who were graduating that year. It sought advice concerning their desire to do missionary work and asked for the support and encouragement of the association. This presentation was followed by a testimony from each of the four. A committee was appointed to consider their request. This led to the formation of the American Board of Foreign Missions.

MARRIAGE AND ORDINATION

That same day Adoniram was invited to eat at the home of deacon John Hasseltine. He saw Hasseltine's daughter Ann helping serve. She was about twenty. Her dancing eyes and vivaciousness attracted him. Adoniram secured Hasseltine's permission to seek Ann's hand, telling him that he must realize that he planned to take her to India, never to come home again. He talked about the hardships, persecutions, and the possibility of violent death she may suffer for the sake of perishing souls.

The father, with many misgivings, left it to Nancy (the name Ann always went by) to make up her own mind. Her mother hoped she would not accept but did not withhold her consent. After two months of courtship, Nancy accepted him, fully aware that no woman had ever left America to be a missionary.

On September 24, 1810, Adoniram received his M.A. from the seminary.

Shortly thereafter, on January 11, 1811, Adoniram sailed for Britain in a British vessel, but during the voyage the ship was captured by a French privateer. Adoniram was crowded with others into the filthy hold of the ship. In France, through the help of an American, he escaped from the jail, saw some of the sinful life of France, managed to get to Paris; in May he arrived in Britain. He appealed to the directors of the London Missionary Society and worked out a conditional agreement for British-American cooperation. After six weeks in England he returned to America and reported to the American board. The four young men were then appointed as missionaries in Asia or wherever God led them.

Things began to move very rapidly. An ordination service was arranged. Donations began to roll in. Missionaries were prepared to go out, planning never to return. Adoniram and Nancy were married on February 5, 1812. They had a farewell service in her church the same day, and the next day the candidates were ordained. A death-like hush fell over the service, for it had an aspect of farewell. The whole congregation was moved to tears.

To India

On February 19, 1812, the sailing ship *Caravan* set sail, and 114 days later it reached Calcutta, India. After an unfriendly welcome by government officials, the missionaries visited Dr. William Carey, the pioneer missionary who had founded the London Missionary Society.

Soon the missionaries were taken to Serampore and assigned a large house in which two of the young missionary families—the Judsons and the Newells—were given two rooms each. Because of tensions resulting from the War of 1812, the British ordered them to leave India and forbade them to go to any British dominion or territory.

The Burmese government refused missionary work. Its record was the bloodiest on earth, with the most common punishments being crucifixion, beheading, or pouring melted lead down the throat. Finally, the missionaries received permission to go to the Isle of France (Mauritius), but the ship could take only two people. The other young couple, the Newells, decided to go, because Mrs. Newell was soon to have a baby. In a few days the other ship on which their friends were passengers docked with four more missionaries.

Adoniram stayed for a time in their home and studied Baptist theology books. Nancy was not in favor of him studying these books but began to study what the Bible had to say about baptism by immersion for herself and eventually became one with him in belief. They arranged to be baptized by the Serampore missionary William Ward, coworker of William Carey, on September 6, 1812.

To Burma

The Judsons kept exploring possibilities of where they could serve the Lord. Adoniram could not get Burma and his desire to translate the Bible into Burmese off his heart. With difficulty they managed to get a ship to the Isle of France. They were alone, and Nancy was pregnant. They decided to go to Penang but would have to go first to Madras, India, to get a ship for Penang. At Madras the only ship available was going to Burma. Nancy employed a European woman as a servant to help her when the baby was born. But before the ship sailed the woman had a seizure and died. In a few days Nancy went into labor, and the baby was stillborn. Three weeks after leaving Madras they were in Rangoon, a dirty, disappointing city.

In a few days Adoniram found a teacher. He knew no English and Adoniram knew no Burmese, but by diligent efforts they made progress. Nancy became more fluent in everyday Burmese, while Adoniram worked on grammar and religious vocabulary.

After two years the Judsons received their first mail. They learned that the Baptists in the United States were forming local missionary societies, so more prayer would uphold them.

The Judsons would need those prayers, for baby Roger was born on September 18, 1815, but the next March he died and was buried in their garden. Adoniram also suffered from poor health.

In October 1816 the Houghs arrived. Mr. Hough was a printer and printed a tract for Adoniram and some pages of Adoniram's translation of the Gospel of Matthew. Adoniram finished his translation of Matthew in May 1817 and began to work on a dictionary of the Burmese language to enable missionaries and others in their work.

THE FIRST CONVERT

Adoniram heard that there were a few Christians in Chittagong, ten or twelve days sailing north of Rangoon. He thought it would help his work to have several Indian Christians nearby to prove that Christianity was not just a white man's religion. He hoped to persuade some of the Chittagong Christians to move to Rangoon. It was difficult to get passage to Chittagong, but he heard that a ship was going there and back shortly, so he boarded it.

As soon as the ship was out to sea, it was struck by tremendous winds and the captain decided to go to Madras, India, instead. Adoniram came down with a severe fever and almost died. The weather was not favorable for the trip to Madras, so he ended up three hundred miles from Madras and had to be carried for days in a palanquin. He found no ship would leave for Rangoon for some months. It was April when he arrived, but it was July before he found a ship. When he reached Rangoon he had been gone for seven months.

During Adoniram's absence, cholera had broken out for the first time in Burma, and people hadn't known how to deal with it.

When Adoniram regained his health, he purchased land and built a structure for church services. Soon the first convert was baptized on June 27, 1819, seven years after the Judsons had sailed from the United States.

In a desperate attempt to get the new emperor to grant them permission to teach and evangelize, Adoniram and another missionary, James Colman, took more than a month-long boat trip up the Irrawaddy River to Ava. Their petition was quickly rejected, and they made the return trip. But all was not lost. Others insisted that they were believers and wanted to be baptized. Now there was a church of ten believers.

TRANSLATING THE NEW TESTAMENT

Nancy's health was very poor, and Adoniram had to take her to Rangoon for better medical treatment. They encountered more inquirers there, and Adoniram gave himself to translation of the New Testament. He finished the Gospels and John's epistles and worked on Acts. He sent Nancy to Calcutta, and she went on to America.

Dr. and Mrs. Price, a new missionary couple, arrived from the States, but Mrs. Price soon died of dysentery. Dr. Price was a skillful eye surgeon. The emperor asked to meet him, so Adoniram went along as an interpreter. The emperor wanted Price nearby and gave him a place where he and Adoniram could live. Adoniram witnessed to the half-brother of the emperor and to anyone else who would listen. Once the emperor asked him to preach to the royal court.

Adoniram returned to Rangoon and again gave himself to translation. By July 12, 1823, he completed the New Testament and wrote a twelve-part summary of the Old Testament. When Nancy returned in restored health after an absence of twenty-seven months in America, their trip up the Irrawaddy River to Ava was like a second honeymoon, and Nancy shared with Adoniram all the news from the States. In Ava they had to stay on a boat for two weeks while a brick house was built for them.

WAR WITH BRITAIN

The Judsons attended the lavish dedication of the new royal city. Shortly thereafter the English attacked and captured Rangoon. When Adoniram reached Rangoon, he found that of his eighteen converts, most had been scattered and their houses destroyed. The Americans were suspected of being spies for the English.

On June 8, 1824, a dozen or more Burmese men led by an official burst open the door of the Judsons' home and bound Adoniram in an excruciatingly painful way and dragged him away first to the palace, which was used as a court, and then to the death house. Three pairs of iron fetters were riveted to his ankles. He fell down on the dirt floor, his clothing tattered, his face grimy. He was given a spot in the corner. His eyes adjusted to the dim light, and he could see about fifty persons in the room, including his foreign friends. Some of the prisoners were already near death. The stench almost gagged him.

At night a long bamboo pole suspended from the ceiling by block and tackle was lowered and run between the fettered legs of the prisoners and then raised again so their feet were in the air and only their shoulders touched the floor. Adoniram's arm was sore from the cut of the cord, and his feet were raw from the heavy iron fetters on his elevated feet. At daybreak the bamboo pole was lowered to about a foot from the floor. Once a day for about five minutes the prisoners were taken out to the prison yard to relieve themselves.

At 9:00 every morning Adoniram's servant brought him a little food from Nancy. Others were similarly helped. Once a week kind Burmese women brought some food, and the men rolled it in leaves to try to save it, but it soon began to rot and added to the stench.

DEATH AND TORTURE

Much of the time the prisoners were forbidden to talk. At 3:00 each afternoon two executioners would come and summon two prisoners for execution. The rest knew they had at least another twenty-four hours to live.

Nancy bribed officials to let her see Adoniram. She was allowed to stand outside the death house door to talk with him, but he was unable to walk and had to crawl to her. She could hardly recognize him. She burst into tears but soon controlled herself to exchange a few words with him. Then she was roughly ordered out and went weeping.

Earlier Nancy had been interrogated at length by Burmese officials, and her Bengali servants had been put in stocks. She had bribed the guards for their release. Now back at home she buried much of the silver she had in the yard, and in another spot she buried the New Testament manuscript Adoniram had translated. The next day she was interrogated again. She did not lie but allowed God to guide her answers, and she was able to retain some of their belongings.

After some weeks Nancy's efforts persuaded officials to move the foreign prisoners to an outer prison. Adoniram was even given a private small hut. But on March 1, 1825, each prisoner was given two more fetters—five per leg—and was moved to the inner chamber of the death house.

On May 2, eleven months after their incarceration, all the foreign prisoners were taken out of the prison and driven like cattle two by two. Adoniram was ill and had not eaten that morning. The outside temperature was over 100 degrees Fahrenheit. His feet were so tender that walking on the hot, burning sand caused him great pain. His feet blistered and after one mile became raw. Every step on the sand left his bloody footprint, and he and all but one of the other prisoners collapsed.

Nancy finally found where the prisoners were and went there the next day. She traveled by boat and cart to the Oung-Pen-La prison, which was eight miles from Ava. She found Adoniram practically in a stupor. Again the prisoners' feet were hoisted, and a cloud of mosquitoes feasted on their feet. The next morning the jailer let them go outside for a few minutes, but only one of the now seven (one had died) was able to do so.

Little Maria Judson was born while Adoniram was in prison. Nancy brought her to see him. Soon after, Maria came down with smallpox. Nancy came down with dysentery and became so weak she could hardly walk. She took a cart to Ava to get medicine and better food. She retrieved the medicine chest she had kept with the governor, took two drops of laudanum at a time, then returned home by boat and cart and crawled back to her home and collapsed.

Nancy was too weak to nurse baby Maria, so she bribed the jailer to let Adoniram out of prison for a time each evening, and he went from house to house in the village, carrying Maria in his arms, begging Burmese mothers who had nursing children to let Maria nurse a few minutes at their breasts. Some days Adoniram was permitted to spend an hour or two with Nancy. Adoniram became very discouraged, but somehow they all lived on.

These sufferings for Christ and for Burma did not stop either Adoniram or Nancy. Their consecration was not short-term. They were committed until the day when God would take them home. They did not have frequent or quick correspondence by letter, and there was no other means of communication available. They did not plan or even think of missionary furloughs or "rest and recuperation" in their homeland. All for Jesus was the commitment of their lives.

Loving Jesus supremely, carrying his vision and love for Burma, and his determination that the Burmese people be a significant part of the bride of Christ in eternity, they pressed on "until death."

Adoniram Judson ———

Part 2: Victory Despite Suffering

Surviving the Death Plan

Adoniram Judson was still in the Oung-Pen-La prison in Burma when the rumor came that the new governor planned to kill all the foreigners, offering them as a sacrifice of victory to defeat the British. But he lost favor with the emperor, and on May 28, three days before the sacrifice was to be made, the governor died. He had been dragged through town, beaten, and then trampled to death by elephants.

The prisoners survived, and so did the Judsons. In August they were taken to Amarapura, and each was given a copy of the British document discussing terms of peace. Adoniram was released on November 4 and was ordered to go to Maloun, where the peace negotiations were in progress, to serve as a translator.

Adoniram arrived at Maloun almost dead with fever, and at times he lost consciousness. He was in a delirium for two days and was too weak to move, but his mind became clear, allowing him to translate the many papers that were brought to him. He had to teach the Burmese how nations handled agreements and contracts.

Finally, a treaty was signed, and he was taken back up the river to Oung-Pen-La.

While the Burmese had been using Adoniram as a translator, Nancy, without his knowledge, had become seriously ill with cerebral spinal meningitis. When he returned home he could hardly recognize his daughter or Nancy because they were so thin and haggard.

A Truce at Dinner

Early in 1826 the British began to advance up the Irrawaddy. All Ava panicked. Adoniram; his eye surgeon friend, Dr. Price; and two captured Englishmen were asked to translate the English demands. The English refused to change the terms—surrender of the captured leaders of Arakan, Tenasserim, Assam, and Manipur, and the equivalent of one million British pounds sterling. The Burmese tried to get the English to bargain. Finally, when the English were only a few miles away, the Burmese melted gold and silver vessels and took silver bars worth only one-fourth of the demanded amount by boat to the English. Adoniram was the delivery person.

Adoniram returned to tell the Burmese that all the foreigners wanting to go to the English must be publicly questioned and all the money must be given at once. A flotilla of six to eight boats carrying the foreigners and the funds went down the river to the English steamboat *Diana*. It was the first steamboat the Burmese had ever seen, and it terrified them. The Judsons were treated like royalty by the English commander. A few days were spent working out the details of the treaty. Then a gala dinner was prepared for the signing.

English flags and banners were flying everywhere, and a regimental band in full uniform played. Sir Archibald Campbell was elegant in his uniform. He took Nancy on his arm and led her to the place of honor. The Burmese, especially the leader who had treated Adoniram so badly, trembled violently. For a year and a half Nancy had had to abase herself before him, begging for money. Now she was being treated as the guest of honor.

Nancy told Campbell how she and Adoniram had been treated by the man, how he had snatched her silk umbrella from her hand and made her stand in the hot sun until noon. With difficulty the English officers kept their tempers in check and remained silent as she told her story. The Burmese could not understand, but they could read the looks on the officers' faces. Perspiration covered the chief Burmese official's face, and he continued to shake uncontrollably. Nancy said to him softly, "You have nothing to fear," as she showed the forgiveness of Jesus.

DOUBLE DEATH

The Judsons settled in the new British center the British had built at Amherst, and Nancy began a school for the children. Three days after they arrived Adoniram left for Rangoon for two months. Then he accompanied a British delegation to Ava, escorted by twenty-eight British and fifteen Indian men. The Burmese tried week after week to change their part of the settlement treaty. On November 24, 1826, a Burmese man arrived with a letter sealed in black. "I'm coming to inform you of the death of your child," he told Adoniram. But when Adoniram opened the letter, he discovered it was Nancy who had died a month earlier, on October 24, 1826.

Adoniram was almost totally convulsed by sorrow for some time. It was overwhelming to realize that Nancy was dead. Little Maria had also suffered from a weak body. Earlier the wife of another of the missionaries had helped the Judsons with her care, and now she took complete charge of her until Adoniram could be informed and could come home. Six months after Nancy's death, Maria was buried at her side. She was two years and three months old.

Adoniram threw himself into his translation work, but he struggled with the shadow of loneliness and gloom. Then in July his father back in Massachusetts died. His father had had such ambitions for his son. In his loneliness, Adoniram began to wonder if his life had been more motivated by ambition than by love for the Lord. He began to read the writings of Madame Guyon, Fénelon, and others. He also practiced self-denial and sought humility. In time his melancholy began to leave him.

Adoniram wrote, hand printed, and distributed only to those who requested them ten thousand gospel tracts. Some people traveled two to three months' journey to ask for them.

FRUIT AT LAST

A new missionary couple, the Boardmans, began work among the Karens, a tribal group who were much more responsive than the Burmese. But Mr. Boardman contracted tuberculosis, and in 1831, while on a trip to work among the Karens, he died. He had baptized thirty-four before he died. His wife, Sarah, continued to teach at a school and make short evangelistic journeys among the Karens.

It had taken nine years to win the first eighteen converts. Now in five years, 242 Burmese and 113 foreigners had been baptized.

THE BIBLE TRANSLATED

Adoniram was now the senior of the missionary group. He knew the Burmese language and people better than anyone else.

All through 1832–33 Adoniram worked on translations of the Burmese Bible. He isolated himself from others to be uninterrupted, and he finished the New Testament on December 15, 1832. Printing the New Testament and other gospel literature had become a major work. Adoniram was not content to translate from the English; he used the Greek New Testament and Hebrew Old Testament. By January 31, 1834, he was able to complete the Old Testament, and he felt released from the burden he had carried for years.

A SECOND MARRIAGE

A few weeks later Adoniram received a letter of congratulations from Sarah Boardman, who had remained in Burma after her husband died. Gifted and skillful in the language, she had gone through the tiger-infested jungle from one Karen village to another with the gospel. She was thirty and he was forty-six. They were married on April 10, 1834, after a four-day courtship. It had been eight years since Nancy had died and three years since Boardman had died.

Adoniram and Sarah made language their main ministry. He suggested that since she was expert in Burmese and Karen, she learn the Taling language and translate into it from the Burmese. Sarah also organized women's prayer meetings, classes, and other women's work. Adoniram preached a sermon each night and preached to a crowded assembly on Sunday. He met before breakfast each morning with his Burmese assistants, guiding their ministry and encouraging them. The church now had ninety-nine members and was still growing.

THE REVISED BURMESE BIBLE

Adoniram completed a revision of the Old Testament on September 26, 1835. A month later, Sarah gave birth to Abigail Ann. At the end of March 1837 he completed a revision of the New Testament. A week later, April 7, 1837, a son was born, Adoniram Brown Judson; and on July 15, 1838, another son, Elnathan, was born.

Adoniram developed a cough and sore lungs, and in February 1839 he was sent to Calcutta on a sea voyage to renew his health. He improved for a time but could preach only once a week. On December 31, 1839, a fourth child, Henry, was born.

On October 24, 1840, Adoniram sent the last sheet of the Burmese 1,200-page one-volume Bible to the press. He felt quite satisfied with the New Testament; he had been revising it for twenty years. But he still was not totally satisfied with the Old Testament.

Adoniram felt that part of his life's work was done, but still not all of Burma was open to missionaries. Now he must give himself to strengthening the Christians and praying open the door to all of Burma. His coworkers urged him to give his time to a good Burmese dictionary that could help everyone, including future translators.

HEALTH BATTLES

On March 8, 1841, Sarah gave birth to a stillborn boy. All the children had whooping cough at the time, and before they were over that, they became very ill with dysentery. Sarah also became ill. By June the doctors told Adoniram that the only hope of keeping his wife and two older children alive was a sea voyage, so they all boarded a ship sailing for Calcutta. It was the monsoon season, and the ship almost sank.

Reaching Calcutta, Adoniram took the family to Serampore, but the heat was so oppressive and the winds so strong the children relapsed. Little Henry (one year, seven months) died. Again the doctor urged Adoniram to take the family on a sea voyage to save their lives. It was an exceedingly stormy voyage to Mauritius, and two sails with their masts were blown away. Adoniram evangelized the crew, and all but two made a commitment to the Lord. He later baptized four of them.

Sarah had three more children—eleven in all (three by Boardman—one who lived) and eight by Adoniram (of whom six lived)—and worked some at translating *Pilgrim's Progress* into Burmese. In 1845 she went down the coast for a while to try to improve her health by a change of climate but returned in two months unimproved.

In an attempt to save Sarah's life, Adoniram broke his resolution never to return to America. They left the three smallest children behind, each with a different missionary. The youngest, only four months old, was nursed by a missionary along with her own baby. With Sarah and the three oldest children, Adoniram sailed for America, taking along two Burmese helpers so he could continue to work on his dictionary.

SARAH'S DEATH

When they reached Moulmein (in modern South Myanmar), Sarah was so much better they decided she and the three children could go on alone and hopefully return in a few years. But she suddenly suffered a relapse, and Adoniram knew there was no alternative to accompanying her. When the ship neared St. Helena, Sarah died. The captain and Adoniram took Sarah's body onshore in a small rowboat, and a wooden coffin was secured in the town. Four esteemed women carried Sarah's body to a spot beneath a banyan tree, where she was buried. As soon as Adoniram and the captain reached the ship again, it sailed on. It was a long, sad voyage to America.

"Mr. Glory-Face"

When Adoniram and the children stepped off the ship, crowds of people were waiting to receive him. The life of his first wife had been read about by several hundred thousand people, and the sufferings he had endured were well known. Thousands had prayed for him. His lungs were so bad he could hardly speak, but the presence of God so transformed his face that someone called him "Mr. Glory-Face."

Welcome service followed welcome service. Many people wanted to interview him. He felt almost suffocated and longed to have quiet times alone. He arranged for two of his children in one home and the other in another home. Then he received word that his son Charlie had died in Burma.

A Third Marriage

Adoniram traveled to Philadelphia with a minister friend, who borrowed a book for him to read while the train was held up by an accident. The book of short articles was written by Fanny Forester, which was actually a pen name for Emily Chubbock, a widely acclaimed writer of children's books. Adoniram was greatly impressed by her style and quality of writing. He asked if she was a Christian. Yes, his friend said, she was a Baptist. And to Adoniram's surprise, she was a guest at the minister's house where he was taken.

Emily was supporting her parents by writing. Adoniram asked if she would write a memoir of his wife Sarah. She was glad to do so, for as a child she herself had longed to be a missionary. Within a few weeks Adoniram proposed marriage to her. He was fifty-seven and she was twenty-eight.

At first they faced a storm of criticism—such a venerated, mature missionary marrying such a young lady! Yet on June 2, 1846, they had a quiet wedding. He visited and said farewell to his three children, and on July 11, with the tears and good-byes of hundreds at the wharf, they sailed. He would never see his native land or children again.

BURMA AGAIN

Emily wrote vivid descriptions of all the interesting things they encountered on the voyage and of their arrival in Burma. She was a keen observer, interested in everything, and was a great joy to Adoniram. She was also a good sailor and enjoyed the four-month voyage. It was the happiest trip Adoniram had ever taken.

As they neared Amherst, where the ship docked, a welcoming party of the new Christians came out in a small boat. It was all so strange, so new to her. She must be brave. How can she cope with all that God had in store for them? Emily went into the cabin and wept, but Adoniram prayed in her ear, calmed her, and she went to sleep. After three days they were rowed up the river to Moulmein. Emily took Adoniram's two young sons, Henry (the second son so named) and Edward, to her heart.

Adoniram did not feel they were needed in Moulmein, for there were now thirty missionaries there. Instead, he went to Rangoon to see if he could make suitable arrangements to work on his dictionary. He stayed there ten days and met the governor, who promised a location for an English church. But he was not to contact the Burmese about Christ. He rented a place to stay, returned to Moulmein, had about a week to pack, and then took the family back to Rangoon.

The Judsons' new home was the upper floor of a large building with huge rooms and innumerable bats. They called it "The Bat Castle." After seven months, government intolerance, lack of food, and sickness drove them back from Rangoon to Moulmein. Their baby girl, Emily Frances, was born. Both felt unusually well the next year, and 1847 was the happiest year of Emily's life.

Besides working on the dictionary, Adoniram was the general overseer of the mission's work, and he preached each Sunday. He became noticeably mellower and more affable, took time with his children, and held meetings for the twenty children of the mission. On January 24, 1849, he finished the English-Burmese part of the dictionary (six hundred pages)—a tremendous accomplishment.

Emily had been weak and delicate in 1849, but her health improved. Now Adoniram developed a severe racking cough, dysentery, and fever.

DEEPER LOVE, DEEPER VICTORY

Adoniram began spending more and more time in prayer. He told Emily that "for forty years he had been trying to love everyone as much as the Savior had enjoined. He had tried again and again, and failed again and again. For forty years he had considered it a sin to love himself, to have feelings of pride."[1] He had suffered unspeakable injustice and had seen the Burmese unjustly treated by their government. He had been willing to forgive as Christ taught. But did he love these brutal men who abused those under them? Did he experience what John Wesley used as a term for the deeper holy life—"perfect love"? He felt he still had inner resentments and knew that holy love should cleanse these away. He had prayed about it repeatedly over the years.

> Then one day in January 1850 [Adoniram] lifted his head from the pillow and told [Emily]: "I have gained the victory at last. I love every one of Christ's redeemed, as I believe he would have me love them.".... He said at last: "And now I lie at peace with all the world, and what is better still, at peace with my own conscience. I know that I am a miserable sinner in the sight of God, with no hope but in the blessed Saviour's merits; but I cannot think of any particular fault, any peculiarly besetting sin, which it is now my duty to correct. Can you tell me of any?" Emily could not.[2]

From then on Adoniram enjoyed a satisfying sensation of great peace. But he began to weaken physically, was lethargic, and slept much more. The doctor advised a sea voyage to regain his health. Emily was expecting another baby soon and could not accompany him. They talked of the possibility of his death. He said:

> Lying here on my bed, when I could not talk I have had such views of the loving condescension of Christ and the glories of heaven as I believe are seldom granted to mortal man.... I am not tired of my work, neither am I tired of the world. Yet

when Christ calls me home, I shall go with the gladness of a boy bounding away from his school. Perhaps I feel something like the young bride, when she contemplates resigning the pleasant associations of her childhood for a yet dearer home—though only a very little like her, for there is no doubt resting on my future....

Death will never take me by surprise—do not be afraid of that—I feel so strong in Christ.... I leave myself entirely in the hands of God, to be disposed of according to His holy will.[3]

Shortly before Adoniram was carried on board the ship, he said to Emily, "I never was deeply interested in any subject. I never prayed sincerely and earnestly for anything, but it came. At some time—no matter at how distant a day—somehow, in some shape—probably the last I should have devised—it came."[4]

Adoniram's Final Voyage

April 3, 1850, was the day Adoniram was carried onto the ship. Emily was able to spend some time each day with him until April 6, when the ship sailed. One of the missionary men was assigned to accompany him. His life had been filled with separation and suffering. Now, again, he was apart from his loved ones. At the end he held the missionary's hand, gently pressing it from time to time. Several of the ship's officers gathered outside his cabin door to watch. At last, at 4:15 on April 12, 1850, he breathed his last on earth.

The crew lined up on deck and silently slid his coffin into the sea in the darkness. They were a few hundred miles west of Burma. On April 22, two days after Emily had received word of Adoniram's death, she delivered her second child, who died at birth.

The next year Emily returned to America with the three children. She prepared the biographical details of her husband's life, and three years later, on June 1, 1854, she died of tuberculosis. Two of Adoniram's sons became ministers and one a physician, one was permanently disabled in the Civil War, and one daughter became headmistress of an academy.

Adoniram Judson was the first American missionary to go overseas. He paid a costly price of repeated, almost unbelievable suffering yet kept his face set unwaveringly forward for Christ and Burma. What a hero of the Cross!

Dwight Lyman Moody —

Hungry-hearted Soul Winner

When Dwight Lyman Moody went to heaven on December 22, 1899, God had used him to reach by his spoken word or pen more people in more places than anyone who had ever lived before him. He had evangelized at least 100 million people and had probably personally dealt with some 750,000. He often addressed anywhere from 40,000 to 70,000 people a week, and at times 10,000 to 20,000 gathered to hear him. One writer said Moody had reduced the population of hell by at least a million souls.

THE UNLIKELY SOUL WINNER

Perhaps no one has ever been such an unlikely candidate for God to use mightily than Moody. He was born February 5, 1837, into poverty. His father died praying on his knees when Dwight was four. The family of nine children went to Sunday school, and his mother read a brief devotional and prayed with the children each day, but Dwight seemed to learn little. His total education was not more than five years of primary school. His penmanship was barely legible, and his writing was filled with misspelled words and grammatical errors.

When Dwight's father died, creditors seized everything, even the firewood, and the children had to stay in bed until school time to keep warm. They were so poor that the brothers would carry their shoes and socks when they walked to church to save them from wear. When Dwight was ten he and one of his brothers went to a farm thirteen miles away to work. At seventeen he tired of farm work and went to Boston without any money. He almost despaired before he secured employment.

Dwight did not feel at home among the well-dressed, more cultured city folk. He was awkward in actions and speech, and he stumbled over words when he tried to read. In later life his friend Charles Spurgeon joked that Moody was the only person who could pronounce "Mesopotamia" in one syllable.

Dwight was won to Christ by his Sunday school teacher at the age of eighteen. He immediately tried to join the church but understood so little about the Bible or salvation that after church leaders questioned him, they put him on probation for six months while three of the board members explained the Bible to him.

Yet Dwight never became a student. He was too active and restless to become a great reader. He loved his Bible and read it constantly but was comparatively unconcerned about theology, current events, or contemporary trends. His grammar and pronunciation always remained conspicuously defective.

SUNDAY SCHOOL EVANGELISM

Two years after his conversion, Dwight moved to Chicago and became a shoe salesman. He also rented a pew in the Plymouth Congregational Church and filled it with young men he invited from boarding houses and street corners. Soon he had rented four pews and filled them every Sunday.

Dwight then found a small mission Sunday school on North Wells Street and offered to teach a Sunday school class. They already had sixteen teachers, and only twelve children attended. He was told that he could be a teacher if he provided his own students. The next Sunday he arrived with eighteen ragged boys from the streets. Soon he had the building overcrowded. In 1858 he began a larger Sunday school mission in another section of Chicago, and that large hall was soon crowded too.

Dwight rented a still larger hall and soon filled it with neglected street children. The average attendance was around fifteen hundred. They loved Dwight, crowded in, and sang enthusiastically. Children began to be saved, parents were drawn in, and Dwight began holding services almost every night of the week. Six years later this was formed into an independent church, out of which Moody Memorial Church eventually was formed.

Dwight's lack of learning and polish was obvious to everyone. Even the street urchins he invited to Sunday school considered him uncouth. Back at the Plymouth Congregation Church, when in zeal Dwight had spoken up one day, one of the deacons told him he could best serve the Lord by keeping silent. Another praised his zeal in filling the pews but told him it would be better if he didn't attempt to speak in public. "You make too many mistakes in grammar," he said.

"I know I make mistakes, and I lack many things, but I am doing the best I can with what I've got," Dwight replied. Then he bluntly asked, "Look here, friend, you've got grammar enough. What are you doing with it for the Master?"

Despite these shortcomings, Dwight was self-confident, energetic, and astute in business. He constantly burned with vision. He did well enough as a salesman to save up seven thousand dollars in four years. He became engaged at twenty-two to a sixteen-year-old teacher of one of the classes in the Sunday school he had started. They were married three years later. His wife was more refined than he and after their marriage helped him make up for his lack of education. Throughout life Dwight tended to be blunt and impetuous, but his absolute integrity, tender spirit, and love for others won him acceptance and respect.

Seeing Dwight's zeal, integrity, and successful work, several well-known Christian businessmen in Chicago, including John Farwell, a partner of Marshall Field, and Cyrus McCormick, inventor of the reaper, began to take an interest in him and help him with funds.

FULL-TIME MINISTRY

Dwight felt the spiritual opportunities were so great that in 1861 he gave up all business work to give himself full-time to Sunday school and YMCA work. Through the YMCA he held evening prayer meetings for adults, Friday teas, English classes for immigrants, daily noon prayer meetings, and a citywide tract campaign. For four years he was the president of the Chicago YMCA. He became a popular speaker at YMCA conventions and had a four-month itinerary representing the YMCA in the British Isles. In the meantime he carried on his Sunday school activities and organized a church.

During the Civil War, Dwight became a prominent member of the Christian Commission, an organization that provided printed materials (Bibles, religious tracts, library books, and religious newspapers) and other goods (such as blankets) to soldiers and prisoners of war. He was extensively involved in this work both in the Chicago area and on many of the battlefields in the southern states. He distributed tracts wherever he went and ministered to both Union and Confederate soldiers. He held eight to ten services every day, and Sunday was almost one continuous service. Many prisoner-of-war camps were in the Chicago area, and hundreds of dying soldiers were led to Christ as he and his helpers prayed with them. Often even before he said the amen, the new Christian was rejoicing in Christ. Heaven seemed so near.

After the war Dwight went back to his Sunday school and YMCA work. His Sunday school was the second largest in the United States and made him nationally famous. People traveled thousands of miles to study his methods. He was called to speak at area-wide Sunday school conventions in many places. Through his efforts many Sunday schools agreed to unite in using the same series of lessons, and out of this was born the Standardized International Sunday School Lesson Series used by thousands of churches and still in use today.

DAILY NOON PRAYER MEETINGS

The daily noon prayer meetings in Chicago dated back to the revivals and the time of Charles Finney in 1857–58, when noon prayer meetings were held in several thousand cities and towns across America. The Chicago noon prayer meetings had dwindled down by this time, until sometimes only three or four people were present. Dwight revived them, and such large crowds began to attend that Dwight raised $100,000 to build a large auditorium—Farwell Hall—in which to hold the meetings. It seated three thousand people and had a separate prayer room for a thousand. It also had a library, reading room, tract and publishing department, relief department, and a private prayer closet. It was dedicated in September 1868.

IRA D. SANKEY

At the Indianapolis YMCA convention in 1870, Dwight met Ira David Sankey, president of the Newcastle, Pennsylvania, YMCA, and heard him sing for the first time. A Christian since age sixteen, Ira was a revenue collector and son of a state legislator. Characteristically, Dwight announced to Ira, "You will have to quit your job. I have been looking for you for the past eight years." But Ira was hesitant to quit the security of his substantial government salary.

The next day Dwight asked Ira to meet him at a certain street corner in Indianapolis. When Ira got there, Dwight was setting up a barrel on the sidewalk. Dwight told Ira to climb on the barrel and start singing. Before he knew it, Ira found himself on the barrel singing "Am I a Soldier of the Cross?" Soon a crowd of factory workers on their way home gathered around him and stayed to listen to Dwight's sermon. It was not long until Ira resigned his job and became Dwight's partner in the Chicago ministries. From then on until Dwight's death, God blessed mightily the Moody-Sankey team across America and the British Isles.

Ira had a strong voice that carried a great distance. He also played a small folding reed organ wherever he and Dwight went in crusades. One of Ira's most famous hymns was "The Ninety and Nine." In Scotland the churches sang only psalms, no hymns, and did not use a musical instrument. Yet Ira's Spirit-anointed singing won them over. In order to have hymnbooks with the kind of songs he and Dwight wanted in their meetings, Ira edited a hymnbook. This Moody-Sankey hymnbook has sold seventy million copies, and its successor volume has sold well over fifty million more. It is still used in Britain.

FILLED WITH THE SPIRIT

Dwight's first visit to Britain was in 1867, as he wanted to study the methods used in Christian work there. He especially delighted to hear and meet the famous English minister Charles Spurgeon. He also met the renowned man of faith George Müller and saw Müller's faith orphanages in Bristol. During Dwight's time in Dublin, after an all-night prayer session with twenty pastors and evangelists, Henry Varley said to him, "The world has yet to see what God will do with and for and through a man who is fully and wholly committed to Him." Dwight determined, "I'll be that man."[1]

The year 1871 was a crucial year for Dwight spiritually. He was a tremendous worker, but, says Dr. R. A. Torrey, his helper and successor, "He had no real power. He worked largely in the energy of the flesh."[2] God used two faithful Free Methodist women to lead Dwight to the Spirit-filled life for which he longed.

Sara Anne Cooke and her widowed friend Mrs. Hawxhurst sat on the front row of Dwight's church every service. While he preached, they prayed, as he could clearly see. Then at the close of each service, they would come up and greet him and thank him, saying, "We're praying for you." This exasperated Dwight, and he said, "Why don't you pray for the unsaved?" They quietly answered, "We are praying that you may get the power."

This perplexed Dwight. Here he had about the largest church in Chicago, and the work seemed to be booming. Surely God was blessing him. But the ladies prayed on. After two months an over-powering spiritual hunger affected his soul. He went to them and said, "I wish you would tell me what you mean." They testified to him and prayed with him that he might be filled with the Holy Spirit.

Dwight testified, "There came a great hunger into my soul. I did not know what it was. I began to cry as I never had before. The hunger increased. I really felt that I did not want to live any longer if I could not have this power for service."[3]

The women kept praying. One Friday as they prayed together, Dwight prayed, "Lord, baptize me with the Holy Spirit and fire." Two nights later, October 8, 1871, the great Chicago fire swept across much of the city, and Dwight's church and home and the homes of many of his people were burned down.

Dwight was devastated. He went to New York to raise money for a new church building and for relief work. As he walked down Wall Street praying, suddenly God answered his prayer for the baptism of the Holy Spirit, and the power of the Holy Spirit fell upon him. Dwight hurried to the house of a friend and asked for a room where he could be alone.

Dwight stayed in that room for hours alone with God. The Holy Spirit flooded his soul with power and joy again and again until at last he asked God to hold it back or he would die on the spot from joy. Dwight left that room with the power of God upon him and filling him.

What was the result? Dwight said, "I went to preaching again. The sermons were not different; I did not present any new truths; and yet hundreds were converted."[4] He added, "May God forgive me if I should seem to speak in a boastful way, but I do not know that I have preached a sermon since but God has given me some soul. I would not be back where I was four years ago for all the wealth of the world."

Torrey tells that over and over Dwight would say to him, "Torrey, I want you to preach on the baptism of the Holy Ghost." Torrey added, "Time and time again, when a call came to me to go off to some church, he would come up to me and say: 'Now, Torrey, be sure and preach on the baptism with the Holy Ghost.'"[5]

IN THE BRITISH ISLES

Shortly after his infilling with the Spirit, Dwight left for Britain intending not to preach, but he was prevailed upon to preach Sunday morning and evening in a London church. Marianne Adlard, a bedridden girl in London, had read in a British periodical about work done among ragged children in Chicago by a man named Moody. She began to ask God to send this man to her home church even though she was never able to attend services herself. One Sunday when her sister came home from morning worship, Marianne asked if anything unusual happened in church that day. She was told that they had a guest speaker from America by the name of Moody. At once Marianne began to pray for the night service, refusing her noon meal. That night the Spirit of God gripped the people and several hundred received Christ. Meetings continued for ten nights, and more than four hundred new members were received into the church.

These services launched Dwight into a tremendous ministry across the British Isles the following year, 1873, when he returned with Ira. Beginning with an almost unparalleled campaign in York in the church of Reverend F. B. Meyer, the campaign moved north across England, Scotland, and Ireland and south again across England to London. Dwight returned to the United States in 1875. In a little more than two years he had become the world's leading evangelist.

For the next twenty-four years God worked mightily through Dwight. He founded a girls' school and then a boys' school near Northfield, Massachusetts. He also founded the now well-known Moody Bible Institute in Chicago and the Bible Institute Colportage Association to blanket the nation with reasonably priced gospel literature.

The results of Dwight's 1880 campaign across England, Scotland, and Ireland and to the universities of Oxford and Cambridge exceeded those of his campaigns five years earlier. In his last British campaign in 1891–92, he preached in more than one hundred places and spoke three to four times each day.

After Dwight's return from Britain he put forth a plan for a multifaceted evangelistic campaign to reach the two million people of Chicago. His emphasis was on prayer and evangelism. He gathered his students and teachers from his schools at Northfield and Mount Hermon at 6:00 A.M. one day "to seek the anointing of the Holy Spirit." With tear-filled eyes and choking voice, he pleaded with them, "If you think anything of me, if you love me, pray for me that God may anoint me for the work in Chicago. I want to be filled with the Spirit, that I may preach the gospel as never before. We want to see the salvation of God as never before."[6] Dwight was so loved and respected around the world that his call for prayer was heeded in America, Britain, Sweden, and Germany. Special days were set aside for people to humble themselves and pray.

The World's Columbian Exposition, or World's Fair, was held in Chicago, Illinois, in 1893 to commemorate the discovery of America in 1492 by Columbus. Dwight caught a vision of a massive, coordinated citywide campaign for Christ to be held at that same time. He arranged for twenty-four leading American pastors, twenty-five famous American evangelists, forty European Christian leaders, and a number of singers, Christian college leaders, and his own Bible Institute students to minister in the campaign.

Dwight used many kinds of meeting places all over the city—church buildings, empty store buildings, theaters, five large tents, and gospel wagons. His team held as many as seventy evangelistic meetings in one day and held meetings for the deepening of the spiritual lives of Christians as well. Dwight said, "Oh, we cannot lead others nearer to Christ than we are living ourselves, and there is no use working unless we are filled with the Holy Spirit. We want to get down on our faces and humble ourselves at His feet. Let us search and try our thoughts, and see if there be any wicked way in us. If we do these things, then our preaching will be with power and our work will bear a precious harvest of souls."[7]

Within four weeks God was pouring out his blessings. Thousands attended on week nights and as many as seventy-one thousand came on Sunday. One Sunday morning eighteen thousand stood in sweltering heat. The crowd was hushed. "Silence became intense; Pentecost came down, and hundreds were saved."[8]

The meetings continued from May through October. Each night the workers returned to Moody Bible Institute to report to Dwight and get their orders for the next day. They called these sessions together "the Holy of Holies." One report said, "Christians came to Chicago from all over the world. . . . Many received the baptism of the Holy Spirit (Moody's term for the fullness of the Spirit). . . . Others were stimulated . . . and fires of revival have been kindled everywhere."[9]

Long after midnight on November 1, 1893, Dwight was at last alone and fell on his knees, sobbing aloud his love and thanks to the Lord. He quoted Simeon, "Now lettest thou thy servant depart in peace, . . . for mine eyes have seen thy salvation" (Luke 2:29–30).

Dwight continued to conduct campaigns around the United States over the next few years.

In mid-November 1898, Dwight went to Kansas City for what proved to be his last campaign. He preached for five nights to crowds of fifteen thousand. He felt his body collapsing. He had done his best. He leaned over the pulpit and pointed his finger upward as he had done hundreds of times over the years, and said, "Good night! and I'll see you in the morning!"

Friends carried Dwight to a train, ironically one whose engineer had been saved through Dwight's preaching. Dwight reached home, weary in body. "He had done his human best, filled with the Holy Spirit."[10]

Then, on December 22, while loved ones stood around his bed, he said in a clear voice, "If this is death, there is no valley. This is glorious. I have been within the gates, and I saw the children! Earth is receding, heaven approaching! God is calling me!" He whispered to his wife, "You have been a good wife to me." And he was home at last. He was sixty-two years of age.

WHY GOD USED MOODY

In a message preached one time at the New York Hippodrome, Dwight said,

> God has got a good many children who have just barely got life, but not power for service. You might safely say, I think, without exaggeration, that nineteen out of every twenty professed Christians are of no earthly account so far as building up Christ's kingdom; but on the contrary they are standing right in the way, and the reason is because they have just got

life and have settled down, and have not sought for power. The Holy Ghost coming upon them with power is distinct and separate from conversion. . . . I believe we should accomplish more in one week then we should in years if we only had this fresh baptism.[11]

When Dr. C. I. Scofield, editor of the famous Scofield Reference Bible, spoke at Moody's funeral, he gave four reasons why God used Dwight. (1) He was clearly saved. He had a definite experience and knew it. (2) He believed in the divine authority of the Bible. To him it was the voice of God. (3) He was baptized with the Holy Spirit, and he knew it. It was to him as definite an experience as his conversion. (4) He was a mighty man of prayer and believed in a mighty God.

A Man of Prayer

R. A. Torrey says Moody was a far greater man of prayer than he was a preacher. Time and again he overcame insurmountable obstacles through prayer. He wanted every campaign saturated with prayer and called for his Bible Institute students to support his ministry with prayer. Often they prayed until the early hours of the morning, and many of their lives were transformed through prayer. Dwight used to arise each morning at about four o'clock to read his Bible and pray.

A Passion for Souls

Dwight burned with compassion for the lost. Shortly after he was saved he made a resolution to speak to someone about his or her soul every day of his life. If he forgot to witness to someone during the day, he would get out of bed at night, dress, and go out into the street to find at least one soul to speak with about Jesus. Once he stepped up to a man standing by a street light and tried to win him to the Lord. Within a few days that man was saved. Another night he saw a man with an umbrella in the pouring rain. Dwight ran up and asked, "May I share your umbrella?"

"Certainly," said the man.

Dwight asked, "Have you any spiritual shelter in the time of storm?"

Dwight walked up to another stranger and asked, "Sir, are you a Christian?"

"Mind your own business," the man replied.

"This is my business," said Dwight.

"Well, then, you must be Moody!" the man exclaimed.

One night Dwight was seen sitting in a shack at the edge of a city where he was ministering. A young black boy was on his knee and a candle was in one hand as he helped the boy read the Bible.

One day in Chicago when Dwight was doing his Sunday school work, he spotted a little girl some distance away. He had previously invited her to Sunday school, but she had not come. Dwight started toward her, and she began to run. Dwight ran after her, down one street, up another, through an alley, into a saloon, out the back door, up the back steps, and into a room upstairs over the saloon. The little girl crawled under the bed. Dwight pulled her out by the leg and led her to Jesus. Then he led the poor widow mother and the other children in the family to Jesus. They all became faithful members of his church, and years later that little girl became the wife of one of the leaders of the church. Said Torrey, "When Mr. Moody pulled that little child out from under the bed by the foot, he was pulling a whole family into the Kingdom."[12]

That was Moody—always hungry for souls, always compassionate, always willing to be a fool for Christ, always praying and digging into God's Word, always humble. Always he emphasized that every Christian needed to have a definite experience of being filled with the Holy Spirit. One night after some teachers argued against such a definite experience, Moody turned to Torrey and said, "Oh, why will they split hairs? Why don't they see that this is the one thing they themselves need?"

Why doesn't everyone?

Evan Roberts

Chosen for Revival Ministry

Who was Evan Roberts, the young coal miner and blacksmith God chose to light revival fires across Wales and much of the world? Evan was born June 8, 1878, the ninth of fourteen children. Eight of these were alive at the time of the Welsh revival. As a child Evan always wanted to help others and make them happy. He was very unselfish and would do work around the house that he thought would save his father time.

THE PRAYING CHILD

Evan would get other children to pretend they were holding a religious service, and he would be the leader of the group. He memorized many of the hymns in the Calvinistic Methodist hymnbook. As far as possible he attended every meeting held in the church—worship, prayer meeting, and Sunday school. He was constantly hungry for spiritual things. From the time he joined the church at the age of thirteen, he developed a habit of meditating on the Word of God. Often while meditating he would forget everything else going on around him.

Evan's piety had such a silent influence on the other children in the family that, although they were unconscious of it, they respected him even more than their beloved parents. The children would say, "We must be quiet—Evan is coming." He was never harsh or severe with them, but if anyone in the house spoke in a way of which he disapproved, one glance from his eye, without a word, would quiet them.

As far back as Evan could remember, he always loved the Lord and was not sure of the date of his conversion. He said that though he knew the Lord he was not conscious of God's love burning in his heart until after he was filled with the Holy Spirit. But all those years he hungered to do more for Jesus. He was a great lover of nature and saw God in all of nature. The spring flowers on the hillsides spoke to him of Living Water flowing from the heart of God to quench the thirst of sinners. The mountains spoke of the immutability of the Trinity. The beauties of creation spoke to him of endless variety and of God's own nature. When he looked at the sun, he was reminded of the Son of Righteousness. In fact, he often broke into joyous laughter when he saw the sun. The extensiveness of creation reminded him of the infinity and omnipotence of God. All of nature seemed to remind him of spiritual realities. Some of his sweetest memories were of creation revealing God to him.

A LOVER OF GOD'S WORD

The Roberts family was very faithful religiously and was spiritually minded. The Bible was the subject of their conversation around the hearth. Every day of his youth Evan's father, Henry, memorized a portion of God's Word. Thus, he knew much of the Bible by heart. Evan's mother, Hannah, also loved the Bible, and by the time Evan began to be used of the Lord, she had memorized large portions of it.

Henry's untimely death when Evan was twelve necessitated Evan getting work in a local coal mine to help support the family. From the time he began working in the mine, he was daily loving God, hungering for more of God, and trying to obey him. He prayed almost constantly and above all else cried to God with two main requests: "O God, fill me with your Spirit" and "O God, send mighty revival."

While Evan worked, he was almost constantly singing, praying, and repeating Bible verses. He kept his Bible in the mine with him and read during the lunch break while others played cards. In the blacksmith shop he kept his open Bible near at hand. Arriving home in the evening, he would read his Bible for hours. He usually read it while he was eating. He also read Bible commentaries and theology books. He loved to pray on his knees and often lost track of time while in prayer. From the age of fifteen Evan was appointed a Sunday school teacher and Sunday school secretary. Soon he was made superintendent of the Sunday school. Then he was also asked to lead the singing. He learned to play the piano and organ as well. Evan also enjoyed writing hymns on the Holy Spirit and poetry expressing spiritual truths.

A Life of Prayer

Evan could not remember a time when he did not pray. From childhood on, praying was as natural to him as breathing. He considered prayer the most powerful influence in his life. He prayed at home, while walking along the road, and at work. He often preferred spending time in prayer over sitting down to eat a meal. When he arrived home from work hungry, he would nevertheless always go to his room to commune in prayer for a while before he ate.

Often after others went to bed Evan would spend time, sometimes hours, in prayer. After he went to preparatory school, he would often spend more than half the night on his knees in prayer, mainly in silent communion. The school principal said he had never heard anyone pray with such hunger and agony as Evan. Again and again, lost in prayer, Evan would call out, "Oh!" in deep soul burden.

At times during the revival Evan would stand in the pulpit and pray silently at length, even as much as one and a half hours at a time. Sometimes his whole body would become weak and he would stand in the pulpit leaning on his Bible and praying with deep longing sighs. His life goal was to be in prayer continually.

Evan often sensed that other people were praying for him. He would become lost in prayer, almost as if he could hear their prayers. Later he would sometimes discover that many were praying for him at the very time he sensed they were.

Evan longed for the Holy Spirit to be poured out in worship services and believed that the success of a meeting depended directly on the amount of prayer for it. At times he stopped people from singing and told them that prayer was more important. He said, "We may sing all night without saving. It is prayer that tells, that saves, and that brings heaven down among us. Pray, friends, pray."[1]

Evan became deeply convinced that God planned to use him across Wales in some way, but he was unqualified educationally to attend a Bible college, so he enrolled in a preparatory school. Yet he found concentration difficult because of his prayer burden.

FILLED WITH THE SPIRIT

On October 29, 1904, just two weeks after he entered the school, Evan was one of twenty young people who accompanied Reverend Seth Joshua, the main evangelist of the Forward Movement in Wales, to Blaenanerch to attend his meetings. On the way they sang:

> It is coming; it is coming; the power of the Holy Ghost.
> I receive it; I receive it; the power of the Holy Ghost.[2]

At a 7:00 A.M. service Joshua included these words in his closing prayer: "Bend us, O Lord." As they went out for breakfast, Evan prayed, "O Lord, bend me." The Holy Spirit said to him, "That is what you need." God deeply moved Evan in the 9 A.M. service by the words "God commendeth his love" (Rom. 5:8). The Holy Spirit came upon him mightily. He fell on his knees, perspiration pouring down from his face and tears streaming from his eyes. For about two minutes he cried out, "Bend me, bend me, bend me! Oh! Oh! Oh! Oh!" He felt God's love bending him and visualized the lost bending before God on Judgment Day.

The prayer Evan had been praying constantly for thirteen years was answered, and he knew he was filled with the Holy Spirit. "I felt ablaze with a desire to go through the length and breadth of Wales to tell of the Savior," he said.[3] As Evan prayed those days, he envisioned a team of his young friends going with him across Wales in an evangelistic campaign. God gave him a vision of a hundred thousand being won for Christ. He kept exhorting people to pray for the Holy Spirit, to surrender absolutely to and to obey the Holy Spirit. He kept speaking of the revival he was sure God was going to send. He wrote, "The divine fire has begun to lay hold of us." *Total surrender* was a term he used repeatedly.

Evan gave every day to God, and God came mightily upon him as he prayed. One night he could not sleep because of the power of God's presence. He reported, "The room was full of the Holy Spirit. The outpouring was so overpowering that I . . . had to plead with God to stay His hand!"[4]

VISIONS

God also gave Evan visions during his prayer time at Blaenan-erch. In one vision he saw the vast fiery pit of hell surrounded by a wall with one door. He saw a surging mass of people coming as far along the horizon as he could see, all heading toward the pit. He pleaded with God to shut hell's door for one year.

In another vision Evan saw Satan in a hedge, deriding him and laughing in defiance at him. Then he saw a glorious white figure with a flaming sword held high. The sword struck the figure of Satan, who instantly disappeared. Evan knew Christ was going to defeat Satan.

Another time Evan saw a brilliant moon and then an arm stretched out to the world. Again he saw the vision, and this time the hand held a piece of paper on which was written "100,000."

The next night, Sunday, October 30, while in a service, Evan had one more vision. He could see the schoolroom in his own village and his young friends and companions sitting in rows before him. He could see himself speaking to them. One person clearly stood out. That person proved to be the first one moved on by the

Spirit when Evan began his meetings in Loughor. He heard God's voice say, "Go and speak to these people." At last he said yes to God, and instantly the vision vanished and the whole chapel seemed filled with light and glory.

That Sunday a minister preached on the text, "Father, glorify thy Son, that thy Son may glorify thee." Evan became so absorbed in God's presence that he was aware of nothing else. One of his friends reported, "I could not see the face of Roberts; those who could see it told me that his face was shining, his countenance was changing, and appeared as if under a wonderful influence."[5]

On Monday morning, October 31, Evan received the principal's permission to leave the school for a week. When he arrived home his family was bewildered by his behavior. He talked of being greatly blessed, of being baptized and filled with the Spirit. When he thought of the need in Wales, he would burst into tears and weeping, but when he thought of God's promise of revival and souls, he would laugh for joy. He said to his brother Dan, "You shall see there will be a great change in Loughor in less than a fortnight. We are going to have the greatest revival that Wales has ever seen." At the table he said to the family, "We must believe God and His word. . . . there will be wonderful things here before the end of the week."[6]

God sent revival that began that Monday night, October 31, in the schoolroom adjoining the Loughor church and continued that week in services at Loughor or in another nearby chapel. It soon spread in South Wales and in North Wales. Evan's thirteen years of prayer for revival along with the prayers of many others had been answered.

The revival fire the Holy Spirit lit that night leaped from country to country, and within two years' time some five million people were converted and joined the churches. It was not by might, nor by power, but by God's Spirit (Zech. 4:6).

Two of the first five converts of that revival, Henry and John Penry, took me to the old schoolhouse where the revival began. "There's where I was sitting when the fire fell," said Henry, who had been one of the thirteen young people there that night. Later we were praying in the old Moriah chapel. While kneeling in prayer with Henry and John after they testified how God had come in the 1904 revival, Henry prayed, "Come suddenly again, O Lord." I began the following poem while he was still praying and while we were on our knees and finished it after concluding with prayer myself.

COME SUDDENLY
(Malachi 3:1)

Come suddenly again, O Lord;
Your temple waits for You today.
Come in accordance to Your Word;
Come suddenly e'en while we pray.
O blessed, blessed Holy Ghost,
Bring the revival we need most.

Most graciously our hearts prepare
For Your great work in this our day.
Help each of us to do our share;
Remove each hindrance from Your way.
O Holy Ghost, our hearts inspire;
Descend in all Your holy fire.

We need You more than we can tell;
We need You more than we can say.
Our worldliness and sin dispel;
Come, cleanse and fill us all, we pray.
O Holy Ghost, come on us now
As we in need before You bow.

We pray Lord, light the flame once more
Of Holy Ghost revival fire.
Come now as in the days of yore;
For You we wait with great desire.
Come suddenly upon Your own
And make Your holy presence known.

Come suddenly and do much more
Than we can do in months and years.
We plead Your mercy o'er and o'er;
We praise You that revival nears!
Come, Holy Ghost, descend today!
Come suddenly on us, we pray.

—*Wesley Duewel*[7]

HOLY RADIANCE

Evan was five feet eleven inches in height, slender, vivacious, and swift of movement. He would often swing his long arms as he spoke. He had an intense desire to see sinners saved, and as the meetings began, he wept over the lost. When he communed with God his face would shine in such a way that the people around him all noticed it. It "shone with an unearthly luster, as Moses' face must have done when he descended from Sinai."[8] Often he was so full of joy that he did not seem to notice the things about him. When Evan asked others to pray with him, they seemed immediately filled with a spirit of prayer and praise and felt perfectly natural kneeling with him. They too seemed to forget time and were caught up in the spiritual reality.

Evan avoided criticizing people and instead praised them. He loved his friends, prayed constantly for them, and was ready to sacrifice anything for them. He would not even say a discouraging word about his antagonists. He constantly reminded people of Jesus.

If a topic of conversation did not please Evan, he would begin to talk about the miraculous works of God and his saving of sinners and would begin to laugh until all would be filled with joy. Whenever he heard of the conversion of a great sinner, he would laugh and say, "Thanks be to God!" Often tears would immediately stream from his eyes.

GUIDED BY THE SPIRIT

Evan constantly depended on the Spirit's guidance in accepting invitations, in attending services, or even in participating in services he attended. He did not go to Cardiff, where thousands were waiting, because he felt checked by the Spirit. He wanted to be in the background and leave all the glory to Christ. In some places crowds were absent at first, but since Evan knew God had sent him, he persevered. Soon there were many and powerful conversions in these places.

Evan always spoke quietly with no attempt to impress people. He sought as far as possible to remain in the background, except as the Spirit urged him to give an exhortation, pray, or give some other form of leadership. At times when he stood in the pulpit he would be absolutely silent, and then someone would break out with an agonizing prayer of confession of sin. Others would follow one right after another. People would be kneeling in pews, in the aisles, all over the church. Then hymns of joy would start. Sometimes a morning service would last all day long. News would reach other churches, and the service would become a neighborhood revival.

A London journalist who attended the meetings was amazed at the way the meetings flowed almost without human leadership or direction. Singing, Scripture reading, prayer, testimonies of converts, and brief exhortations by different people all succeeded one another as the Spirit led. Evan exhorted continually, "Obey the Spirit," and the Spirit kept the meeting peaceful and in holy order.

AN OVERWHELMING SENSE OF GOD'S PRESENCE

In some services young people and children outnumbered adults. In fact, one newspaper reported that in general two-thirds of the congregations tended to be men and half of those were young men. Children between nine and twelve years of age prayed with great anointing and maturity, to the amazement of congregations. Again and again in services hours passed like minutes. People lost all sense of time and were only aware of God's presence and the Spirit working in lives. One minister was amazed as he left a service to discover he had been there for ten hours. He said it had only seemed like ten minutes, and he found the church still surrounded by hundreds of people waiting patiently to get inside.

They had been there throughout the entire night. A hush was on them all because God's presence had overwhelmed them.

The revival went on in power with people praying, testifying, and seeking God; the old, formal way of worship seemed almost impossible. Churches were crammed night after night, week after week, as the revival fire burned on. In some places soccer and rugby matches had to be canceled because everybody was so involved in the revival.

The revival swept like a sea wave from mining valley to mining valley across Wales. Often revival began and hundreds were converted even before Evan arrived at a given place. A newspaper reporter visited one mine and at seventy yards from the bottom of the shaft found a group of eighty miners listening to a workman read Matthew 6, reading by their dim lamp lights. Then they sang, shouted amens, and one miner after another led in prayer until it was time to begin work. Evan went to the mine pit heads to greet the men as they left the mine. He would shake hands with each one and invite him to the meetings. Most came. The transformed miners added energy to the singing in the services and fervency in the praying.

Many churches, hearing about the revival in South Wales, were led by the Spirit to hunger for revival in their own towns. The pattern the Spirit seemed to follow was (1) prayer meetings with young people especially taking an active part, and (2) prayer continuing until the Spirit was outpoured. Sometimes these prayer meetings were started by individuals, sometimes by church leaders or even by the entire presbytery. Smaller visitations of revival fire appeared in various other parts of the British Isles.

In the first five weeks of the revival, 20,000 conversions were recorded. Newspaper reporters would attend the services and count the number of people who would arise and testify to being born again. From November 8 through December 31, 34,131 had been born again. At the end of the first four months, newspapers listed 83,936 people who had been saved. This was not by any means the total, because many villages did not supply the number converted.

A WORLDWIDE IMPACT

The Wales revival was reported at some length and with photos by the press in many nations—even Roman Catholic nations like France, Italy, and Portugal. People arrived in the Welsh villages by train from all over the British Isles and from other countries. At times Indians, Chinese, Japanese, Germans, French, Americans, and Russians could be seen in a small village church, and when the Spirit would grip them, prayer in several different languages could be heard simultaneously. Local residents showed the visitors generous hospitality by inviting them into their homes.

Prayer requests were sent in from many nations, and Evan believed that God would spread the revival fire throughout the world, and God did—even in India, Korea, North China, and Latin America.

When asked the secret of the revival, Evan replied, "I have no secret. Ask and ye shall receive."[9] Again he said several years later, "It is certainly beyond my power to instigate a fresh revival, for revival can alone be given by the Holy Spirit of God when the conditions are fulfilled."[10]

A LIFELONG MINISTRY OF PRAYER

By the autumn of 1905 Evan's ministry and influence waned. He felt physically exhausted and in April 1906 retired to recuperate in the home of Mr. and Mrs. William Penn-Lewis in England. From 1907 on he gave himself almost exclusively to the ministry of intercession. In February 1932 Evan wrote, "My work is confined to prayer, and it is to such that I have devoted myself for the last twenty-five years.... I work as hard at prayer as if I had undertaken any other form of religious work.... By preaching I would reach the limited few—by and through prayer I can reach the whole of mankind for God."[11]

In 1928 Evan had returned to Gorseinon for a short time and fellowshiped with a prayer group of some thirty members. God used him in the healing of some and in the casting out of demons. Evan was very much aware of the conflict with evil spirits and

Satan, as is indicated by the famous book he coauthored with William Penn-Lewis's wife, Jessie, entitled *War on the Saints*.

From 1930 until his death in 1951, Evan lived in Cardiff, South Wales. In Gorseinon his friends told me that occasionally he would come back and sit quietly in one of the local services. In 1964 his last surviving relative, Mrs. Dan Roberts, widow of his brother, over my protest, gave me a page from the surviving fragment of the Welsh Bible Evan always carried to the coal mine when he was a miner. It had been damaged in an explosion at Loughor on January 5, 1897. Her explanation for her insistence was, "You are giving your life for that for which my brother-in-law gave his entire life." (I was at the time editor of a magazine named *Revival* that OMS International was printing in twelve languages.) This assures me that until death Evan Roberts interceded for the work of the Holy Spirit and revival.

(I wrote the following words in Gorseinon in 1964 after a prayer time with the two Penry brothers in the room where the revival began. The brothers—one the song leader, the other the organist—were two of the first five converts of Evan Roberts during the revival. The next time I spoke there, they led the singing of this hymn to the tune of *Stella,* a British hymn tune.)

WE NEED THE SPIRIT

Lord, light again the sacred flame
Of Holy Ghost revival fire.
He Who at Pentecost then came
Is He Whom we so much desire.
We need Him in our midst today;
Oh, send Him to us while we pray.

Revival is Your work, O God;
'Tis for revival that we plead!
Spread holy flames of fire abroad
And meet Your people's deepest need.
Oh, send the Spirit's holy pow'r
Upon our waiting hearts this hour.

We need the Spirit to convict
And bring once more the sense of sin.
May sinners feel their conscience pricked
And see how far from God they've been.
With Holy Ghost conviction seize
'Till sinners fall upon their knees.

We need the Spirit to give birth
By His transforming, saving grace.
May He reveal the Savior's worth;
May He show Jesus' loving face.
May He give fettered souls release;
With all His life and joy and peace.

We need the Spirit to empow'r,
To cleanse and fill and sanctify.
Send Him upon the Church this hour
'Till all their Savior glorify.
Make holy love to overflow;
Set lives and faces all aglow!

Oh, send revival once again;
Lord, set our spirits all aflame!
Reveal Your glory unto men;
Once more exalt Your holy name!
Revival is our greatest need;
Oh, send the Holy Ghost we plead!

—*Wesley L. Duewel*[12]

Girolamo Savonarola ———

God's Shining Revivalist

G irolamo Savonarola was one of the greatest prophetic preachers, reformers, and revivalists the world has ever known. Martin Luther was fourteen years old when Savonarola became a martyr. Savonarola's thundering denunciations of the sins of the Roman Catholic Church prepared the way for the Protestant Reformation.

Savonarola was born September 21, 1452, in Ferrara, Italy. By the express order of Alexander VI, one of the vilest of popes, at the age of forty-six Savonarola was hanged and his body burned in the public square of Florence, the city he loved so well. His parents were cultured but worldly people. His grandfather was an influential physician in the court of the duke of Ferrara, and Girolamo was well educated by his grandfather. He was a very diligent student and soon became proficient in liberal arts and philosophy. He was an earnest student of the writings of Aristotle and Plato.

The writings of Thomas Aquinas fed Girolamo's soul and led him at an early age to yield his whole heart and life to God. His spiritual fervor and devotion began in his boyhood and deepened as he grew older. He would kneel and pray before the altar in the church for hours, until it was wet with his tears, a practice that continued throughout his lifetime. He agonized over the lostness of the world, the shameful corruption of the church, and people's rejection of Christ and his salvation. He knew God was calling him to be separate from the sins of the age and to be a voice for God.

Savonarola was a loyal Roman Catholic, and his life was shaped by the teachings, rites, ceremonies, and the whole religious system of the Catholic church, for he knew no other. Nevertheless, his sensitive soul keenly felt not only the sins of society but also the sins of the church. This awareness filled his days with constant sorrow.

HOLINESS UNTO THE LORD

Everywhere Savonarola saw worldliness, immorality, and wickedness. He was aghast at the contrasts between the luxurious lifestyles of the rich and the abject poverty of the many poor. He burned with zeal for truth, purity, and godliness and was shocked by the shameless sinning of all of society, particularly the lewd, lavish, and at times cruel lifestyle of wicked political tyrants, priests, dukes, and even many of the popes of his day.

Savonarola talked little, often sought to be alone, and continually grieved over the sins of his nation. He frequently wandered along the banks of the River Po singing to God or weeping over the sins of the people. His only comfort was prayer.

Savonarola would go to the church and lie on the altar steps for hours pleading for God's mercy and help against the sins of his age. His hours of weeping intercession prepared God's way for the Reformation. Daily his prayer seemed to increase in fervor. He was disgusted with the world, weary from observing wrongs and blatant evil, so he decided to retreat from the world to a monastery.

When Savonarola was twenty-three years old, while his family was away, he fled to a Dominican monastery in Bologna, Italy. His favorite author, Aquinas, had been a Dominican. He did not ask to become a monk, but to be permitted to do the most menial work. He had left behind in his home a paper he had written entitled "Contempt for the World," likening the world to Sodom and Gomorrah.

A LIFE OF FASTING AND PRAYER

In the monastery Savonarola gave himself to fasting and prayer and to prolonged, intense study of Scripture. He literally pored over Scripture day and night until his soul burned with the intense fire of the Holy Spirit. He knew the Word from beginning to end and quickly surpassed others in modesty, humility, and obedience. Soon he was asked to be a lecturer in philosophy. All the while he grew more grieved and furious at the sin he saw in the Roman Catholic Church.

After seven years, at the age of thirty, Savonarola went to a monastery in Florence, the most beautiful and cultured city in Italy. The rulers of Florence were greatly encouraging the Renaissance, a revival of learning. Most of the people of Florence could read Greek and Latin. Savonarola had high hopes to find purer, more noble lives there, but underneath the culture and beauty he found dissolute, selfish, and sinful lives.

A PROPHET OF JUDGMENT

Savonarola was promoted to the rank of a preacher in the monastery. Even though the library was filled with books, he gave himself more and more to studying and meditating on the Bible. He went to neighboring towns and thundered God's coming judgment on sin, but the people would not listen. In Florence itself sometimes only twenty-five people would come to hear him preach.

Savonarola once attended the General Assembly of the Monks of the Dominican Order held in another city. On the second day there he rose and condemned the sins of the clergy and corruption in the church. His soul burned as white heat, and his eloquent message made a deep impression. His soul cried out against famous eloquent preachers who never condemned the sins of the people.

One day, at the age of thirty, Savonarola was seeking God in meditation and prayer when God gave him a vision that revealed his future judgments upon the church, and a voice urged him to announce them to the people. He felt divinely called from that moment. God clothed him with a new anointing and a mighty empowering of the Holy Spirit.

Savonarola now became God's prophet to the people. He thundered denunciation of sin until people left the services dazed and speechless. Often the whole church was moved to tears and the whole church building resounded with the loud weeping of the people. Men, women, philosophers, poets, laborers—all classes of people burst into passionate tears. Revival had begun.

THE SHINING FACE

Again and again as Savonarola fasted and interceded for the people and the nation he would be caught up in a trance, and the power of God would so come upon him that he would have to retire to some solitary place. On Christmas Eve when he was thirty-four, he sat in the pulpit without moving for five hours, his soul caught up in holy ecstasy, and everyone in the church saw the illumination of God's glory on his face. Such manifestations of God's glory in his countenance occurred on a number of subsequent occasions.

For three years Savonarola preached with great power in a small kingdom in northern Italy. Many were so convicted of their sins that they wept before God. God told Savonarola that a great work was awaiting him in Florence, so in 1489 he returned there.

Savonarola began to teach the book of Revelation to the friars in the monastery. Laymen begged to attend. The meetings had to be moved to the church because of the crowds. People clung to the iron grating to hear and see him. He then had to be moved to a great cathedral, where he preached for the rest of his eight years in Florence.

REVIVAL BEGINS

People became so eager to hear Savonarola that they arose in the middle of the night and waited for hours for the cathedral doors to open. They came along the streets to the church singing and rejoicing. Revival had come. Savonarola predicted the death of the duke, the pope, and the king of Naples all within one year.

His predictions came to pass. As the duke lay on his deathbed, he sent for Savonarola to come and pray with him, for only he had been courageous enough to condemn the duke's sins.

Savonarola had prophesied that a new Cyrus would attack from beyond the Alps to punish the people for their sins. Later Charles VIII, king of France, attacked Italy, captured and looted the city of Naples, and then advanced to attack Florence. People flocked to Savonarola, who called on them to repent. He then went personally to King Charles and urged him to spare Florence, or God would pour out his judgment on him also. Charles remained for some time and then reluctantly withdrew from the city. Savonarola became the hero of the people.

Savonarola now advised the people in his sermons to set up a just government, so they set up a new, enlightened form of democratic government with just taxation, abolition of torture, laws against gambling and excessive interest rates, and major provisions for the poor. For years this form of government served as a model to many nations, and it has continued to influence our modern world.

REVIVAL DEEPENS

God used Savonarola to bring a bloodless revolution and moral and biblical revival. Reformation and revival swept Florence. The city became a praying city. Most of the people attended church and helped the poor. Merchants made restitution for exorbitant prices they had charged. Eminent citizens and scholars became Dominican monks. Feuds were forsaken. Teenage gangsters, street urchins, and bands of riotous youth abandoned their vulgar, obscene songs and began to sing hymns. They formed a "sacred militia." Carnivals and shows were abandoned. Even the city of Florence gave up its traditional revelries. Immoral sex, public gambling, and drinking were forbidden. The citizens abandoned worldly and vile books and instead read Savonarola's sermons. He wanted Florence to become "a city of God."

In 1497 numerous bonfires were lit and indecent and worldly books, pornographic pictures, masks, and wigs were burned.

Children marched from house to house collecting worldly and sinful objects—gambling equipment, cosmetics, false hair, pornography, and lewd books. A great octangular pyramid was made of these in a public square. It was 60 feet high and 240 feet in circumference at the base. People surrounded it holding hands and singing hymns while church bells tolled, and it was burned in a great Ephesian bonfire (see Acts 19:18–20).

At times Savonarola preached to crowds of up to fifteen thousand people—an immense crowd in 1497. When he preached, his words poured out like a torrent, and often people recognized a seemingly divine light radiating from his eyes and face. He taught that all believers were in the true church. His followers were called "the weepers" as they wept over the sins of the people.

The pope tried to win Savonarola over so he would stop denouncing the sins of the pope and his clergy. Then he tried to bribe him to be silent by offering to make him a cardinal. Savonarola refused to stop his prophetic preaching and teaching. He said that Pope Alexander was the representative of Satan, not Christ, and needed to repent. Repeatedly Savonarola had foretold that after eight years of ministry in Florence, he would die a martyr, and he knew that his preaching against the sins of the pope might result in martyrdom. When all the pope's other efforts failed to silence Savonarola, he sent emissaries to Florence to stir up the people and to make libelous accusations against him. He excommunicated Savonarola and threatened that unless the city acted against Savonarola, he would order all sacred acts in Florence to cease—the observance of Mass and public worship, the observance of the sacraments, and all burial rites.

TORTURE AND DEATH

The tide began to turn against Savonarola. The mob that had praised him began to revile him. The pope ordered that he be arrested and burned at the stake. He was arrested, and he and two of his friar helpers were tortured and interrogated for forty days, at times by the papal emissary himself. He was subjected to inhuman sufferings. His hands were bound behind him by strong chains, which were then tied to a rope attached to the roof of the building. He was first drawn up to a great height and then let fall to within a few feet of the floor with great violence. His body, remaining suspended in the air, sprang upward again so that his shoulders were pulled out of joint and his muscles strained and torn. He was insulted, struck, and spit upon. Burning coals were applied to his feet so that his flesh and his nerves were half burned, but he refused to recant. These methods of torture were repeated several times. When he was returned to his cell he would kneel and ask God to forgive his enemies.

Before Savonarola's execution his clerical garb was removed and the bishop stammered, "I separate you from the church militant and the church triumphant." "Militant, yes," replied Savonarola, "but not from the church triumphant. That is not in your power to do." Thousands of people jeered at him, but Savonarola was so absorbed in devotion that he seemed almost unaware of what was going on around him. A priest asked him what he was thinking as he endured his sufferings, and he replied, "Should I not die willingly for Him who suffered so much for me?" An awful silence reigned, and suddenly a coarse voice called out, "Now, prophet, is the time to work a miracle." He and his two companions were hanged and their bodies burned as martyrs for Christ on May 23, 1498. The ashes of the three were cast on the Arno River.

Savonarola was the greatest pulpit preacher Italy has ever furnished. He stood for moral righteousness in private life, in civil government, and in the church. Above all, he was a Spirit-filled, Spirit-anointed prophet and revivalist—God's great gift to Italy and the church of his day. Had Italy been more God-fearing and loyal, it could be that the Protestant Reformation would have begun in Italy instead of some years later in Germany under Martin Luther. Luther called Savonarola a Protestant martyr.[1]

Savonarola did not have the light on doctrine and holy ethics that we have today. He did not have the experiences the Reformation, the evangelical leaders of the church, and the revival movements of the past centuries have taught us. He was not supported by prayer groups or churches. He obeyed God's will as he understood it and stood alone against Satan's power and the engulfing darkness and unbelief. But according to the light he had, he was a fearless prophet condemning sin and proclaiming righteousness, one of the great prayer warriors of Christian history, and a hero of the holy life. His face is said to have glowed with God's radiance many times. May God give us men and women of God with a Savonarola-type commitment for our day.

Amanda Smith —————

Anointed Soul Winner

CHILDHOOD IN SLAVERY

Amanda Smith (1837–1915) was a freed slave greatly used of the Lord. God frequently used her in singing a cappella some of the great hymns of the church and of her black people. He also used greatly her exhortations and messages in homes and in church services and large gatherings. Through her, God brought times of refreshing to many churches and brought about the salvation and sanctification of thousands of people in the United States, England, India, and Africa. She died in Chicago at the age of seventy-eight.

The slave owner who owned her father was unusually kind to him. After he had finished his assigned work, the slave owner permitted him to take on extra work to earn money to buy freedom for himself and his family. He worked almost day and night, sometimes getting only two hours of sleep at night, and was able to purchase his own freedom. But the owner of his wife and children was not at first willing to let them go.

One daughter of the slave owner, Miss Celie, had been cared for since childhood by Amanda's mother. As a young lady she went to a Methodist camp meeting and was saved. Amanda's mother and grandmother had been praying for her salvation. Miss Celie's family now tried to keep them separated, but she would slip away and pray with Amanda's mother and grandmother. They prayed continuously that Amanda's family would be set free.

The slave owner was feeding Amanda to fatten her and prepare her for the slave market, but her grandmother's prayers prevailed. Later the slave owner was about to give Amanda and one of her brothers as a dowry when two of his children were to be married, but again the grandmother's prayers prevailed.

Amanda taught herself to read by cutting out large letters from newspapers and learning to put them together to spell words. The only education Amanda ever had was when she was twelve years of age. For three months in the summertime a teacher taught her during the noon hour and in the evening.

In time, Miss Celie contracted typhoid fever and rapidly worsened in spite of the best available care by four doctors her family secured. For three days she begged her family to permit Amanda's father to buy the freedom of his wife and children. Just before she died she made one more request, and they tearfully promised that Amanda's father would be permitted to purchase his family's freedom.

AMANDA'S CONVERSION

Amanda was married to her first husband, Mister Devine, when she was sixteen. The next year she almost died of severe illness. She was convicted by the Holy Spirit of her sins and once went forward in a Baptist church for prayer but was not saved. She fasted, read her Bible, and in her spiritual blindness prayed to the moon and stars. On March 17, 1856, she desperately determined to be saved. She went down in the cellar, where she often went to be alone for prayer. Three times she got to the end of herself. Finally, she prayed, "O Lord, if You will help me, I will believe You."

As she told the Lord she would, he did. Instantly, peace and joy flooded Amanda's soul. The burden of sin was gone. God's blessing came through her body like a wave again and again. She seemed surrounded by a new light and looked in a mirror to see if she was still the same person. She walked up and down the kitchen floor praising the Lord. For a week she was so happy she did not know what to do with herself. Never again did she doubt her conversion.

Soon Amanda's husband enlisted in the Civil War and died without returning. Amanda then married a local Methodist preacher, James Smith, for she longed to do the Lord's work. Her husband, however, deceived her and dropped all thought of the ministry. He took on employment but did not support her. She supported herself and her children by doing laundry and cleaning houses. Five of her babies died in infancy.

FILLED WITH THE SPIRIT

Several years earlier Amanda had heard that it was possible for born-again Christians to be sanctified and made holy by the infilling of the Holy Spirit. One day a friend came to see her and found her weeping over her condition as she washed clothing in her washtub. Her husband was so hard to please, so unkind. The friend told her, "Well, get sanctified, and then you will have enduring grace."

"My, is that what sanctification means? Enduring grace! That is just what I need! I have always been planning to get out of trials, instead of asking for enduring grace." She began to pray, "Oh, Lord, sanctify my soul and give me enduring grace!"[1]

Often Amanda prayed for sanctification but lacked a clear understanding of scriptural truth. One Sunday after she and her husband moved from Philadelphia to New York City, she was led to go hear Reverend John Inskip, a Methodist pastor and holiness preacher, the first president of the National Camp Meeting Association. God sanctified her during the singing of the closing hymn. In his sermon, Inskip had said, "Get God in you in all His fullness, and He will live Himself."

> Just then such a wave came over me and such a welling up
> in my heart, and these words rang through me like a bell,
> "God in you, God in you." Doing what?, I thought. Ruling

every ambition and desire, and bringing every thought into captivity to the obedience of Christ. The blessedness of love and peace and power I can never describe. The great vacuum of my soul began to fill up, and I wanted to shout, "Glory to Jesus."[2]

But Amanda kept quiet until the last hymn about the cleansing blood of Jesus. Then she could hold quiet no longer and shouted, "Glory to Jesus!" Reverend Inskip responded, "Amen! Glory to God!"[3]

The Spirit began to guide her in many small things, and she sought to obey completely. For a time she was greatly troubled over the doctrine of the Trinity. She did not doubt it but felt she did not fully understand it. She prayed for days. A great renewed baptism of the Spirit came over her, and she realized the fatherhood of God and the brotherhood of Christ as never before. Waves of glory seemed to sweep over her, and from then on the doctrine of the Trinity was clear to her.

A Vision of Jesus

Amanda longed for Jesus to reveal himself to her. Day and night for a whole week her soul cried out, "O Lord Jesus, reveal Thyself." She went about her work praying and weeping and hungering. She so longed to see her beloved Jesus.

One day as Amanda was praying with a close friend, she had a vision of Jesus coming through the door. He was so beautiful, his face so lovely. He came and stood by her side. She heard no audible voice, but Jesus seemed to say to her heart, "Now look at Me. Will that satisfy you?" She cried out, "Yes, Lord Jesus," and threw out her arms to embrace him, and he vanished instantly. She could never forget the glory of that hour.

On another occasion as Amanda meditated on Jesus, his presence seemed so constantly near that she felt he was walking by her side. He talked with her about many things. It was so real she turned to gaze in his face, but no one was there. Psalm 107:9 became very real to her: "He satisfieth the longing soul, and filleth the hungry soul with goodness."

In another vision God laid a heavy marble-like stone cross upon her. She awoke and asked God to explain it. Again she seemed caught up in a dream-vision and she saw people ridiculing her and opposing her. She saw four fierce lions come leaping across the clouds to devour her, but as she called out, "Help, Lord," two great clouds swallowed up the lions. As she turned to go, she heard the most beautiful heavenly singing of a militant hymn she knew well. The singing passed and faded in the distance. This experience helped prepare her to face opposition in the future.

Evangelistic Ministry

In 1869 Amanda's second husband died and she remained a widow thereafter. She continued to do washing and cleaning but barely made enough money for herself and her thirteen-year-old daughter, Mazie. At times she was without food and almost penniless. On one occasion she had only three cents, but she trusted the Lord for everything.

Amanda gained employment at a company but took a stand to attend church each Sunday rather than working, even though the other employees taunted her for doing so. In October 1870 at God's command she gave up her work and began to evangelize. She felt led by God to move to Salem, New Jersey, but she did not have the money. As she prayed, however, God supplied. By faith she went as far as Philadelphia. She witnessed in the streets and saloons, handing out gospel tracts. She visited the sick and began to exhort, sing, and pray in gospel meetings.

Amanda was often overflowing with love and the joy of the Lord, and through her singing she often brought great blessing to church services. She still faced trials, however. She had to combat racial prejudice against "colored" people and against her as a woman. As a black person, she was forced to sit on the top of a bus rather than inside, and she was not permitted off the bus until all the white people were delivered to their destinations first.

REVIVAL

At Salem Amanda had the opportunity to "tell her story" in a night service. Chills ran through her body as she rose to speak, but God anointed her and gave her great liberty as she spoke on Acts 19:2: "Have ye received the Holy Spirit since ye believed?" The Holy Spirit fell upon the people, and some were converted and saved that night. She was permitted to speak again on Thursday night. The church was crowded, and when she gave the invitation the altar was filled.

God gave revival day and night for two weeks, and the revival spread for twenty miles around. Many were converted and others were sanctified. Some people were so convicted of their sins they could not work. Some young men who were converted hired a wagon, drove out into the country, and brought back a load of people to the church. Then, after those people got saved, the young men took them home again.

One night Amanda was too weary to go to the meeting, and a family invited her to their home to visit. She had prayer with them, and five people were converted. The next afternoon she was invited to a house in the country, and revival came there. Five or six people were saved while she was with them. The next day she began to go house to house during the daytime and spoke in the church at night.

After Salem, Amanda went to Millville, New Jersey, where God again worked mightily. She called people to fasting and prayer. People not on speaking terms for months were reconciled. God's power fell upon people "like lightning," and faces shined with the glory of the Lord.

Amanda preached mainly in her own denomination, the African Methodist Episcopal Church. One year she went to Nashville, Tennessee, to their general conference. She paid her own way but with great difficulty found a place where she could rent a room to stay. The entire conference was invited to the Fiske Conservatory. The famous Jubilee Singers were the choir. Their leader spied Amanda in the back of the audience and wanted her to come to the platform to sing. He knew how God blessed her singing, but because of the plainness of her dress, the people tended to shun her. He went back to Amanda and led her to the platform to sing, and the choir joined in the chorus each time. God's Spirit was poured out as she sang. From then on the people accepted her.

Amanda received many invitations from pastors to come to their churches and minister, as well as invitations to many of the holiness camp meetings. Wherever she went she gave her testimony of how God had sanctified her and filled her with his Spirit. She was in great demand to sing hymns and camp meeting songs that seemed to bring the Lord's presence very near.

Amanda always prayed carefully about any invitation before she accepted it. She became loved and respected by many godly ministers and the holiness people in general, as well as by the bishops and leaders of the Methodist church. At times she was given money for travel by those who invited her, but often she had to pray and trust God for funds for the camp meeting fees and expenses.

MINISTRY IN ENGLAND

In 1878 God gave Amanda a very clear sense of guidance and inner conviction that she was to go to England. God supplied her ticket, but she started without the necessary funds, trusting the Lord to provide. She began at the Keswick Convention and ministered in other conventions. Unexpected gifts continued to supply all her needs wherever she went. She was taken to see places important in the religious history of England and Scotland, and she was asked to minister in halls and even in some chapels.

God continued to fill Amanda's meetings with crowds, and many of the services were mixed gatherings of men and women. It was unheard of, especially in Scotland, for a woman to speak to men as well as women, but God showered his blessings on her and continued to save many souls.

MINISTRY IN INDIA

Amanda was invited to India to minister but did not give it a thought until the Lord reproved her for not first asking his will.

Again, God gave her unusually emphatic and clear guidance. She said, "I cannot tell how, but as I waited before Him, He made it as plain as day to me that I was to go. I praised Him and rose from my knees without the least shadow of a doubt in my mind."[4]

Again Amanda did not have funds for the trip, but without any hinting to people of her need, all her funds were supplied. God's promise to her was, "All things, whatsoever ye shall ask in prayer, believing, ye shall receive" (Matt. 21:22). When God whispered this promise to her, she rose from her knees believing that God would prove faithful if she was in his will. Amanda was accompanied by an English friend and was privileged to visit Paris and other parts of France, Florence and Rome in Italy, Alexandria and the pyramids in Egypt, and Bombay, India. She visited the various Methodist centers in India and spoke in place after place. She had a twofold thrust—salvation through Jesus Christ and temperance.

Amanda visited the work in Naini Tal in the Himalayan Mountains in the north. There were tremendous downpours of rain, and on one occasion many houses and buildings were swept away on the crumbling mountainside by the flood. God gave her a tremendous prayer burden, and later she found that one of the missionary men just missed death at the very time she was praying. She continued to minister across India and South India and then moved on to Burma and back to Calcutta.

MINISTRY IN AFRICA

From India Amanda went by ship to the Canary Islands, then on to Liberia, where the Lord blessed her with many souls saved. Then she journeyed on to Sierra Leone, where she ministered wherever she went, at times with Bishop William Taylor. He highly valued Amanda's prayer ministry, sound Bible teaching, and testimony and gladly included her in his ministry.

In Calabar, Nigeria, Amanda saw the darkness of heathenism and the evils of slavery and polygamy existing there. She was caught in a terrible storm off the coast, and death seemed imminent. But as the small ship tossed, God kept bringing to her mind,

"I shall not die, but live, and declare the works of the LORD" (Ps. 118:17). In spite of her desperate seasickness, her soul shouted, "Hallelujah!"

Several times Amanda spent all night or many hours in a tossing, open boat. Sometimes as she prayed the storm would quickly subside. Again and again she would feel great physical weakness, but God gave her strength to go on. At times she would be asked to go to one house after another to pray with sick or spiritually needy people. After several hours of such ministry, she would return to her room trembling with exhaustion. At times when she felt great weakness as she spoke, Amanda testified that she could sense the Lord put his hand behind her back, strengthen her, and hold her steady until she completed her message.

"Blessed be the name of the God," rejoiced Amanda. "How well I know His mighty touch of strength and power."[5] At times Amanda would be asked to hold a street meeting in an area where there were few Christians. The meeting organizers would clean up the street, cut down bushes, set up a small table with a clean tablecloth, and crowds would come. After Amanda spoke, often the Christians would be hungry to be filled with the Spirit and would kneel down right in the street and God would mightily pour out his Spirit upon them.

BACK TO ENGLAND

Amanda had gone to Africa with a strong sense of God's calling and stayed there eight years. She testified that she did not leave "till I was sure I had His sanction."[6] She was so physically ill and weak that she did not think she would live more than three weeks longer. She was almost penniless when she arrived in England in November 1889, but the Lord began to supply her needs through various gifts.

Amanda had the joy of meeting many Christian leaders, such as Mrs. D. Bordman of London; Mrs. Hannah Whitall Smith; Mrs. Mark Guy Pierce; the Crossleys at Star Hall in Manchester, who were leaders of the Salvation Army; Mr. Reader Harris; and a Mr. Morgan, the publisher and editor of *The Christian*.

AT HOME IN THE UNITED STATES

Amanda arrived in New York on September 5, 1890. She ended her autobiography at this point. Her last words were a prayer that God would raise up "younger women who have talent to do better work for the Master" and that after her death they would carry on the standard "with the inscription deeply engraved on heart and life 'Without holiness no man shall see the Lord.'" Wherever Amanda went she was ready to give her testimony of how God had saved her and then filled her with his Holy Spirit. She conducted herself with the simplicity of a child but the dignity of a king's daughter. Wherever she went she emphasized the Holy Spirit, depended on the Spirit's guidance, and sought to lead the unsaved to Christ and the Christians to Spirit-filled victory.

Amanda had a weak body all her life but constantly looked to God for strength, happily endured hardship as a soldier of Jesus Christ, and traveled long distances for Jesus' sake. She was always glad to sing a camp meeting song or hymn, to shout "Hallelujah," and to praise the Lord. In addition to her hundreds of meetings across America over the years, she ministered twelve years in England among the Keswick people and others. In spite of her physical weakness, she lived to the age of seventy-eight, having strengthened the witness and work of Christ wherever she went.

AMANDA'S CLOSING YEARS

After returning to the United States in 1890, Amanda preached for a while and then gave the last twenty years of her life to black orphans. She established the Amanda Smith Industrial School for Black Girls in Chicago in 1899. It was destroyed by fire in 1918, three years after her death. She spent her last years in Sebring, Florida, in a home provided for her by Mr. George Sebring. She died in 1915 of a stroke.

Bishop J. M. Thoburn, a missionary of the Methodist church, thanked God for Amanda's clear vision and faith "which I have seldom found equaled." He said that during his seventeen years in Calcutta he had known many famous speakers to visit the city, "but I have never known anyone who could draw and hold so large an audience as Mrs. Smith." He added, "I have learned more that has been of actual value to me as a preacher of Christian truth from Amanda Smith than from any other person I ever met."[7]

John Smith ———————————

Part 1: Holy Wrestler in Prayer

J̲ohn Smith is an example of a circuit leader in early Methodism in England, who, like the "circuit riders" in America, poured out his life and burned out for God. More than half of the circuit leaders in America died before the age of thirty; John lived to only age thirty-seven. He was well-known in England at the time, but like many of his American counterparts, is little known today.

Without any special campaigns, but with prevailing prayer, he won souls wherever he went—not just a few, but in amazing numbers. There is perhaps no greater example in the history of the English-speaking church anywhere in the world of the winning of multitudes, almost daily, by nothing but prayer and simple preaching in churches. Little is known of Smith's home life, but his wife (they were childless) seemed to be in harmony with his sacrificial burning out for God.

John Smith was born in England on January 12, 1794, not quite three years after the death of John Wesley. His mother and father, who were both home missionaries, dedicated John to God before he was born. At the age of two he nearly died. The doctors said he would not live until morning, but his parents held on in prayer. For six weeks his father prayed almost day and night. John survived, and from his earliest childhood he knew he was called to the ministry. (He said he sensed the call to India at age five and a half while he was playing alone in a sandbox.)

John Wesley was known for spending two hours daily in earnest prayer. John Fletcher, godly coworker of the Wesleys and called by Wesley the holiest man he ever knew, also spent many hours in prayer. But it was John Smith who was called "the preacher with callused knees."

John only lived to be thirty-seven years old. He literally burned out for God winning souls almost every time he preached—and he preached almost every day. At times several score were saved or filled with the Spirit in one day.

SAVED AND SANCTIFIED BY THE SPIRIT

In April 1812 John was born again in his parents' home at the age of eighteen. The next day he read thirty chapters in his Bible and began a lifelong devotion to God's Word. He memorized several of the New Testament epistles and began spending many of his leisure hours in private prayer.

John was cleansed through the infilling of the Holy Spirit in 1816. His biographer said he was "copiously baptized by the Spirit." John believed and experienced that once a person was sanctified he or she could have new outpourings of the Holy Spirit. In his ministry John experienced "many visits from the Lord, especially in private."[1] These were times of personal revival.

WEEPING WRESTLER IN PRAYER

John was early Methodism's holy wrestler in prayer. Often the floor of his study was wet with his tears as he prayed hour after hour for the salvation of souls. He once wrote his parents,

> Blessed be God, He is carrying out His good work in my soul. He has of late poured upon me a spirit of wrestling prayer. He has also astonishingly answered my prayers. I hang upon Him continually, and He keeps my soul in peace.... The Lord

still inclines me to offer and urge a present and full salvation. The Gospel offers nothing less than a full salvation. We want the faith that cannot ask in vain; a holy panting, laboring, hungering, thirsting; and this constantly.[2]

John's example was Jesus himself. He wrote,

> Oh what a happiness to be delivered from *all* anger, peevishness, pride, malice, etc. Let us feast ourselves on Jesus. Let us contemplate Him, our infant Savior in Bethlehem, and be humbled. Let us listen to Him. . . . "The Son of Man hath not where to lay His head," —and be humbled. Let us look at Him washing His disciples' feet, and be humbled. Let us walk with Him in the Garden, view Him prostrate on the ground, sweating great drops of blood, hear Him crying, "If it be possible, let this cup pass from me," and be humbled. Let us behold Him on the cross, and be humbled; yet still let us be confident.[3]

PREVAILING UNTIL THE OUTPOURING OF THE SPIRIT

John believed that prayer was the key to the outpouring of the Holy Spirit. He said, "The work of the Lord is prospering. Glory be to God, a spirit of prayer is given. . . . Oh that God would pour out His Spirit upon us in an abundant manner! . . . Oh, do not cease to cry unto God. . . . Extraordinary effects are not produced by ordinary means."[4]

John also believed that if people were not getting answers to prayer, they had not been praying effectively; if there was no outpouring of the Holy Spirit, they were not pleading God's promises; if people did not seek to lead others to Christ, they had little love of Christ. Any church that remained cold and formal in its praying, weak in its faith, and listless in its love was in a needy spiritual condition. He felt that he was not fully anointed and was unfruitful when people were inadequately praying for him.

MORE AND MORE OF GOD

On April 7, 1818, John wrote his father,

Blessed be God, He is carrying on His work in my soul. Of late, I have had some precious seasons, both in public and private. I want more of the spirit of prayer. There is nothing like getting filled with the Spirit before we go to the house of God, and then pleading with God in the presence of His people.... Last Tuesday night, at the prayer meeting, there were six souls set at liberty. On Sunday night, I preached a funeral sermon from John 9:4. At the prayer meeting afterwards the Lord brought three into liberty, and I believe many others were much affected.[5]

Three weeks later John again wrote his parents,

Of late I have had many visits from the Lord. I can venture on Christ for deliverance from sin; but I want to be filled with all the fullness of God, to have the mind of Christ in me. Oh, urge your members to purity of heart! Much will be done by a single act of faith in the blood of Jesus.[6]

John expressed his heart's constant desire:

Oh, get transforming views of Christ: these you must get in private. Do not rest without the constant enjoyment of the perfect love of God. Get deeper baptisms, signal revelations of the love of God in your heart. Experience the Word, feel that you have the same Spirit that inspired the sacred penman....

Oh, if we were always filled with the Holy Ghost before we go to the house of God we should see signs and wonders.[7]

On December 22, 1818, John wrote,

Let us plead with God for deeper baptisms. We want more of the Spirit. This should be our grand petition,—The Spirit. He will purify, strengthen, comfort, yea, all is in Him. Give God no rest. How soon can He come down and shake the mountain, and dash the rocks to pieces? ... Let us take hold of our fellow creatures (by prayer), consider ourselves one with them, and plead with God for them.[8]

Travailing for Souls

As John traveled from church to church in his circuit he was troubled when souls were not being saved. After visiting one church he noted, "We saw nothing particular. Perseverance; we must have souls converted."[9] John Smith's biographer wrote,

> Where the results which he desired did not attend his ministry, he would spend days and nights almost constantly on his knees, weeping and pleading before God, and especially deploring his own inadequacy to the great work of saving souls. He was, at times, when he perceived no movement in the church, literally in agonies, travailing in birth for precious souls, till he saw Christ magnified in their salvation.[10]

VICARIOUS INTERCESSION

John believed, "When you are with people in distress on account of their sins, you must not only pray for them, but you must throw yourself into their circumstances; you must be a penitent too; they must pray through you, and what you say must be exactly what they would say if they knew how."[11] So he entered vicariously into the sins of others:

> The condition of sinners inspired his heart with an unutterable pity. He entered so fully into their misery and peril, and had so poignant and distressing a sense of the malignity and heinousness of their violations of God's law, as to be often indescribably oppressed. It was a settled principle with him to "confess the sins of the people." "I remember," says Mr. Clarkson [John's close friend], "to have heard him remark, that 'unless a preacher carries about with him a daily burden, he is not likely to see many sinners converted to God.'"

Mr. Calder, John's coworker, testified,

> I have often seen [John] come downstairs in the morning, after spending several hours in prayer, with his eyes swollen with weeping. He would soon introduce the subject of his anxiety by saying, "I am a broken-hearted man; yes, indeed, I am an unhappy man; not for myself, but on account of others. God has given me such a sight of the value of precious souls, that I cannot live if souls be not saved. Oh, give me souls, or else I die!"[12]

SWEETNESS AND LOVE

John loved to visit the sick and saw the need for compassion. He wrote,

> Lately God has signally blessed me in visiting the sick.... My soul has been filled and expanded. The excellencies of Jesus have been more fully revealed. It is good frequently to visit the abodes of the afflicted, especially when Jesus gives us sympathy for the afflicted. I long for more sympathy. I must go to Jesus for it. As man, He was full of it. As God-man, He is the fountain of it. Jesus, come and live in me, that I may, like Thee, go about doing good.[13]

John had such sweetness and kindness that children loved him. His biographer wrote, "Children ... attached themselves to him with peculiar fondness, which he amply returned. In this respect, he resembled the founder of Methodism, and, I may add, the Founder of our holy religion also.... This ceaseless concern for the children and servants of the members of the church was attended with glorious results."[14]

REVIVAL EVERYWHERE HE WENT

John believed that revival was the result of the Holy Spirit's operation, and that faith and prayer would surely bring the Spirit's operation at all times and to an unlimited extent. He once wrote,

> God is one pent-up revival. He breaks forth whenever He can find an instrument that is determined to break what hinders him. Anybody may do it; the lowliest man in the church, the most obscure person, provided that one knows how to pray.
> ... anybody can have a revival who knows how to pray. This truth is well illustrated by the fact that some revivals come as a surprise to the pastor, although usually they travel through his bleeding heart.[15]

John did prevail in prayer, and in every circuit to which he was assigned, from Brighton in 1818 on, God sovereignly gave souls.

John often recorded the spiritual results of revival services in his journal.

> October 7 [1826]—. . . Some scores of people have been set at liberty since I was at Cudworth, and many have obtained clean hearts. During the feast week at Ratcliff I think about thirty souls found peace. Last Tuesday in the prayer meeting five souls were saved. Two years ago we had no society at Hyson; now we have fifty in the church and ten on trial (probation), and a chapel that will hold three hundred people.[16]
>
> March 22 [1827]—. . . God is working mightily among us. I think we have on trial (probationary membership), this quarter, about four hundred and fifty. Laboring, pleading men are increasing. God will stand to His engagement: the work must go on. . . . The last time I was there (Arnold), not fewer, I think, than twenty found peace. God seems to be agitating nearly the whole village. Lenton, which has long been desert, is fresh and green; the society has been more than doubled; Burton, the same. At Bulwell, last Monday night, my very dear father preached. Two were cleansed from sin, and eight or ten found peace. On Tuesday, at Old Basford, one obtained a clean heart, and twelve or fourteen found peace. Glory, glory be to God![17]

A month later John recorded,

> April 24—At Old Basford last Sunday night sixteen or eighteen obtained entire sanctification, and eight were pardoned. At Halifax ten or twelve found peace; and last night two were pardoned and one was cleansed. The work is sure to go on, for God and we are agreed. Labor, labor (prayer) is absolutely necessary.

And nearly a month after that, he had this to report:

> May 19—At Normanton, the last time I was there, twelve found peace. The following evening, after a mighty struggle, twelve were saved. I heard this week that last Sunday and Monday nights thirty were set at liberty. A short time ago I saw nine or ten saved at Epperstone. Last Sunday I was at Mt. Sorrell preaching for their Sunday schools. I think nearly

twenty got liberty and some others were awakened. Glory be to God!

Month after month John recorded such results, and by July 11, 1827, he reported at Old Basford: "Our increase this year is about six hundred, and we have about three hundred on probation."[18]

John Smith continued to keep a record of the powerful move of the Holy Spirit in revival through 1829 when his health was declining. Even when he had to retire from the ministry for periods of time to rest, he prevailed in prayer for souls. And as soon as he was able to minister again, souls came to the Lord almost daily.

Thousands in heaven thank God for the prayer warrior and circuit walker John Smith. If God could use John Smith so mightily, he can use us greatly also.

John Smith ────────────

Part 2: Intercessor for Souls

PAYING THE PRICE FOR SOULS

John Smith longed for and expected souls to be saved and sanctified, and he believed that anyone who paid the price in prayer and faith could see souls saved. In every circuit to which he was appointed he obtained mighty results, with many people turning to the Lord. He believed a Spirit-filled, praying church could expect great results.

John was transferred from Brighton to the Windsor circuit and was married there in 1820. There he had a daily prayer meeting at 5:00 A.M. and another after the Sunday night service. Wherever he served the Lord he was known for "decisive and abundant meetings for prayer."[1] The Lord raised up from the challenge of John's life a group John called "The Praying Men," who stood with him in the prayer battle.

John wrote to a minister friend,

> Be in the will of God. Know that you are in it fully,—constantly. Perhaps you will have to spend hours on your knees, or upon your face before the throne. Never mind; wait. God will do great things for you, if you will yield to Him, and

cooperate with Him. Oh, play the man! Dwell in the light. I am hoping that God will make you a great blessing; but you must be a burning and shining light.... If you spend several hours in prayer daily, you will see great things.[2]

Another price John paid to see souls saved was his health. Some of his friends feared that he was overdoing physically, and while eating at a friend's home they begged him to be more careful. As soon as he was confronted with their concern, John burst into tears and literally sobbed with grief. At length he replied, "What you say is all correct. I ought to put restraint on myself; but, oh, how can I? God has given me such a sight of the state of perishing souls, that I am brokenhearted.... Look around you, my brother; do you not see sinners going to Hell? And when I thus see and feel it, I am compelled to act."[3] In the next few days God worked mightily and about seventy received the assurance of the forgiveness of sins and sixty received heart purity by sanctification.

In the latter part of 1823 John's health began to fail from constant exertion. He went to his parents' home to rest, but when Sunday came he begged the pastor to let him preach, promising to be cautious with his health. In the middle of his message his soul was so ablaze that he forgot and poured out his soul until he almost fell in the pulpit. He again tried to rest, but whenever he resumed his ministry, God used him even more than before.

A severe fever spread through John's community, and he caught it from visiting the people who were ill. He wrote, "Thank God, it has been to me the best affliction with which I was ever visited. It has brought me much nearer to God. I was so touched with the Divine goodness, while in an agony of pain that I was constrained to shout the high praises of God. We had a blessed baptism of the Spirit last night at family prayer. We have devoted ourselves afresh to God, and He accepts us."[4]

A third price that John paid for souls was his time. Almost every week someone convicted by the Holy Spirit came to John's house for counsel and prayer. Sometimes he prayed for up to three hours with such needy ones until they were saved and delivered from their sins and sinful habits. On one occasion the owner of a drinking house sold his place of business and lived a new life in Christ.

SOULS AND MORE SOULS

In one place where John ministered, "there was much of the power of God on the people during the sermon. A special power came down in the last prayer." About thirty were saved that night. Two months later John reported that "the work of entire sanctification is going on in many parts of the circuit. We have a number of private bands and have begun to meet them on Saturday evenings." In one meeting in London eleven were sanctified, and ten of them became leaders. God gave "a blessed spirit" of unity.

John made several visits in the Bath area. At one prayer meeting in the Wolcot chapel, "seven or eight obtained mercy," that is, were born again. On the next evening at the King Street chapel more than twenty were born again, and at a later meeting twenty more.[5]

When John was at home, he would spend several hours in private devotion and then have "family worship" with his wife. This included the reading of Scripture, his comments on the portion read, "the singular sweetness" of family songs, and a time of prayer. After this morning family worship he would go back to his study for private prayer, sometimes on his knees and often on his face. He wrestled with God in intercession until often a considerable part of the floor of his study was wet with tears.

AGONIZING FOR REVIVAL

Shortly after John took charge of the Nottingham circuit in 1825, a friend remarked to him one morning that he didn't look well. He replied that he had spent the whole of the preceding day and night in fasting and prayer, and that he was assured that God was going to bring a glorious revival to Nottingham and its neighborhood. Soon afterward a few friends came to his home one evening and found him in a state of deep depression. He had been meditating on the sinful condition of the townspeople and lamenting their dishonor to God and his laws.

On one occasion John publicly poured forth his sorrows before the Lord, confessing and bewailing the sins of the people with great minuteness and indescribable emotion. His agony was so extraordinary that Mrs. Smith, though accustomed to witnessing his exertions, was unable to endure the sight and withdrew from the room. John's friends rose from their knees and looked at him in astonishment mingled with apprehension. When one of them tried to restrain him and urged him to stop, Mrs. Smith turned to him and said, "'Go, man, kneel down and cry and sigh for the abominations of the people' (Ezekiel 6:11). For nearly two hours he called on God with all his strength. These exertions were accompanied and followed by signs of a coming revival, and in a short time 'there was a great rain.'"[6]

More than 150 were added to the society in three months and more than 220 to probationary membership. During the next three months 200 new members were added and 447 were added on probation. Old members were astonished, having never seen anything equal to it. Souls were saved every week. John wrote, "Numbers [of the members] have trusted God for full salvation, and many more are panting for it. It is the good pleasure of God to save and save fully. How important it is to hold this truth fast through everything."[7]

Two weeks later John wrote, "Many backsliders are returning to the Lord, and cleansing work [members being sanctified] is going on. Last Sunday night at Carlton upwards of twenty, I think, either found peace with God, or obtained a clean heart. We had a still greater night on Monday, at Halifax chapel; and last night, at New Sneinton, many souls were saved. Glory be to God."

No Soul Is Hopeless

John regarded no soul as hopeless. On one occasion an aged dying woman insisted she had made up her mind to be damned. John spent several hours with her, praying and reading passages of the Bible. She kept asking him to stop praying for her, because it was no use—she had sinned away God's mercy. But the more she protested the more zealous he became in his praying. At last she was moved to tears and was saved. In a few more hours she was in heaven.

On another occasion the Holy Spirit was graciously present during a service when a very angry husband entered the door of the church. His wife had begun to respond to the Lord. The husband called out, "Is Mary C... here? If she doesn't come out, I will break her legs."

John stopped preaching and called out, "Lord, lay thy hand on that man, put a hook in his nose and thy bridle in his mouth...." Then he continued his message.[8]

After the message, John spent much time praying with people who had been convicted of their sins by the Holy Spirit. While they were praying the same man entered the church building again. God had powerfully converted him. He had begun to pray, and his wife and another woman from the church had found him gripped by God and had joined him in prayer. God had forgiven him, and he had come back to the church to praise God and testify.

NEARING HEAVEN

As John neared the end of his earthly life, he took refuge in the Scriptures. "The Word of God became increasingly dear to him; his soul seemed to long for its blessed truths, as a parched land for the refreshing shower. The Scriptures, he used to say, were the food of his soul."

On September 24, 1831, just over a month before his death, John wrote,

> "Bless the Lord, O my soul!" The Lord has blessed me exceedingly in body and soul. He has again and again richly baptized me with His blessed and Holy Spirit, and called forth from me songs of thanksgiving. I have had some most delightful seasons in thinking on His adorable name which is a strong tower. I wish to be eminently a minister of the Spirit.[9]
>
> Glory be to the ever-blessed and Triune God, for ever and ever! Amen and Amen. So says John Smith from the very bot-

tom of his heart, which is warm with universal love, love to God and universal men. It is the deep and strong, and, he trusts and hopes, will be the constant and lasting wish of his heart, to get and diffuse as much of God in the world as he can. Who is sufficient for these things? No one, but the men whom God fits for the business. But nothing is too hard for the omnipotent God, who has promised to be with them that seek to promote His glory upon earth. I will try for one, by the help of God. My trust is in a promise-keeping God, whom I wish to adore and worship through endless ages.[10]

In John's last weeks he was often in delirium. Sometimes when he thought he was alone, he called out, "Glory be unto our God! Glory be unto our God!" and his face would light up.

On November 3 several pastors visited John. While they prayed, heaven seemed to fill his room. They began to praise the Lord. John was in his last agony, but his face glowed with sacred joy. He struggled to speak. Summoning all his strength, he whispered, "You said, 'Praise God'; and I said, 'Amen.'" Those were his last words.

Two doctors entered the room. They said John would probably die within an hour. He motioned to know what they said. His friend said, "In less than an hour, sir, it is likely you will be in eternity." A heavenly and triumphal smile came over John's face. He turned his head on the pillow. His friends began to pray, and he was with Jesus. It was November 3, 1831. He was only thirty-seven, but even so, thousands in heaven will call John Smith blessed and thank God for him and his callused knees.

William Taylor

Missioñary Flame

Born in a Home of Revival

William Taylor—the man for whom Taylor University in Indiana was named—was born May 2, 1821, the son of Reverend and Mrs. Stuart Taylor. He was the first of eleven children and was raised in a godly Methodist home in Virginia. His father preached and held revivals for forty years. William was converted at a Methodist camp meeting and later was licensed as an exhorter. In less than a year he was ordained an elder.

William was sent to his first circuit when he was twenty-one. A friend said, "The young man is awfully in earnest, and preaches with power, both human and divine, and can sing just as loud as he likes."[1] William loved open-air meetings. While he was very clear-cut and uncompromising in his preaching of the Word, he was nevertheless also a born diplomat.

William lived on horseback, reading his Bible, preparing his sermons, and praying constantly as he rode. He reported in 1845 en route to a camp meeting, "There, on my horse, in the road, I began to pray more emphatically than ever before: 'I belonged to

God. Every fiber of my being I consecrated to Him. I consent [*sic*] to perfect obedience.'"[2]

EVANGELIZING IN THE GOLD RUSH

William was serving in Baltimore at the time the California Gold Rush began, and his bishop asked him to found a mission in California. William recognized as his commission, "Go ye into all the world and preach the gospel to every creature." He never volunteered to go anywhere or asked for any particular appointment, but he was always ready to accept any appointment. He consulted his wife, and they sailed in 1849 for San Francisco via Cape Horn on a large sailing ship. At that time San Francisco was a city of tents with a few wooden houses built out of packing boxes. There were twenty thousand men and ten women in the city.

William brought with him on the ship precut lumber to build his twenty-four-by-thirty-six-foot chapel, Seaman's Bethel, which became the second Protestant church building in California. Because of the Gold Rush, it would cost five hundred dollars a month to rent a shanty, so William went into the woods, cut down timber, and built his own house. Thus, he became self-supporting almost from the start.

William was pastor to unchurched multitudes, shepherd of the seamen, and guardian angel at the hospitals. He preached six hundred open-air sermons in California among the rough and ready gamblers, sailors, miners, and sinners of all descriptions. Scores of sailors were won to Christ and in turn became witnesses in many ports of the world. William was so mightily used of God during the Gold Rush that he became known as "California Taylor." After seven years in California he preached in the eastern states and Canada. He challenged people to enlist "all the powers of heaven" against "all the powers of hell."

INTENSIVE EVANGELISM

For five years William toured the United States and adjoining Canadian conferences holding revivals and preaching in dozens of camp meetings. One summer he evangelized Philadelphia, preaching in all the Methodist churches. His rule was to travel six days a week evangelizing. Then on Monday night he lectured on California and sold his books. In 1859 he spent almost the entire year in Indiana, evangelizing in almost every town. Wherever he went people were saved and sanctified.

Seldom was William seen on the floor in debate during Methodist conferences. He never sought familiarity with the ranking ministers. He was known for his open-air preaching, his uncompromising but inoffensive methods, and his unquenchable zeal for the salvation of sinners and edification of believers.

ON TO AUSTRALIA

In 1862, while William was preaching in Canada, someone told him of the spiritual need in Australia. He immediately went alone into a nearby forest, knelt in the snow, and asked the Lord if he should go to Australia. He felt led to do so, and on August 1, 1862, he sailed first to Liverpool and then on to Australia. For seven months he evangelized in Britain and Ireland and then went to the Holy Land. His long beard made him look like a patriarch, and Jews and Muslims accepted him almost with reverence.

God providentially guided and anointed William's three years of ministry in Australia. Great revivals ignited, and multitudes turned to Christ. William would hold three Sunday services and emphasize repentance and conversion through Wednesday night and emphasize entire sanctification on Thursday night. Then he would lead a grand rally on Friday night and rest on Saturday. During his intensive three years of ministry, God added eleven thousand converts to the Methodist churches of Australia. Other Christian denominations also reaped good results from his ministry and added new converts.

William's wife surprised him by arriving unannounced in Sydney, bringing their three children with her. He had not seen them for four years. When they arrived, the oldest son, Stuart, was seriously ill, so William went by steamer to join them in Sydney. William had to sit in the lounge with the passengers who were drinking, smoking cigars, playing cards, and cracking jokes, and it was there that he wrote a book on holiness that sold thirty thousand copies.

After arriving in Sydney, William took his family in his arms and wept. He took his two younger sons to a secluded place to pray for Stuart's healing. They wept and prayed together, and Stuart began to get well. The doctor urged William to move him at once out of the Australian heat to South Africa, and he did. God was merciful; Stuart recovered and became part of William's South African team for a few months, leading seekers to Christ.

SOUL WINNING IN AFRICA

William began to evangelize the English, the Dutch, and the Bantu tribal people, using interpreters wherever he could find them. He spent most of his time with the Bantu tribes, challenging them to all-out spiritual conquest for Jesus. He called on them, saying, "Are you going to lie on the shelf? I am not a candidate for 'the shelf.' I am accustomed to sleep in the open sparkling of the stars, and respond to the bugle blast of early morn."[3] William longed to lead thousands more of the African tribal people to the Lord. Even after his retirement he went back to South Africa, and for fourteen more months, until his voice failed, he poured out his life and won many more to Christ.

William went up the African coast by ship, and God gave souls at each stop. In seven months nearly eight thousand people were converted. Many of the church members were sanctified, filled with the Holy Spirit, and set aflame for God. William learned to preach through interpreters, and God gave him a new vision of harvest and revival through black evangelists.

The Dutch Reformed white South Africans were at first horrified that William invited people to come forward to pray for salvation and that he prayed and counseled them during the prayer time. William moved on to King Williamstown, where 600 were converted. In Heald Town God's Spirit was poured out in tremendous power, and in two five-hour sermons 306 Africans and 10 whites were converted. Reported William, "The awful presence and melting power of the Holy Spirit on this occasion surpassed anything I have ever witnessed."[4] It was probably the two greatest days of ministry of his entire life.

William moved on by private conveyance and ministered entirely among the blacks for two months, with his son Charles; his interpreter, Pamla; and another helper. They found intertribal wars, which William calmed; rugged roads; dangerous fords; and treacherous mountain passes. Africans were saved by the scores, and in at least seven cities hundreds were converted. They would come to a new village, and William would call out, "Bring out your men, women, and children and we will sing a song about the country above." They would sing, and then Pamla would announce that at noon the next day the visitor from across the seas wanted to tell them all the good news he had come to tell.

Because God's supernatural anointing on William was so exceptional, he was soon named "The Firebrand" by the native people. He learned that the more gospel he could crowd into a sermon the more powerful the conviction of the Holy Spirit and the more people who were born again.

In England

In 1866 William took his family to England, where he at once began to challenge people for missions and souls. He held one- or two-week campaigns in sixteen Methodist centers in London and a two-week campaign in City Road Chapel, the world center of Methodism. Results were more modest in London, but several hundred were converted.

In Turnbridge Wells, the Taylor family spent a week in the same home with Mrs. Catherine Booth, wife of the founder of the Salvation Army. Mrs. Booth was blessed in the meetings and prayed with the penitents at the altar. One of William's wealthy English friends tried to give him a check for a hundred pounds, but William refused, as he wanted to be self-supporting. From then on, however, the friend periodically gave good amounts to William for his book ministry.

Mrs. Taylor and the children left to return to their California home. They landed in New York, and the train agent, who had known William in his California ministry, immediately gave her and the children free tickets to the West Coast.

WORLD EVANGELIST

William soon left for Bridgetown, Barbados, where God worked wonderfully for three weeks. Then he went to Georgetown, British Guiana. A Methodist conference was in session with some strife and misunderstanding between leaders. God gave William immediate revival and healed the differences, and some five hundred people were converted. Wherever William went, God sent revival. Hearing that his oldest son, Stuart, who had been in school in Lausanne, Switzerland, was again seriously ill, he left British Guiana at once and took Stuart on a Scottish vacation.

In the fall of 1868 Stuart returned to California and William sailed to the West Indies. God used him in revival campaigns in St. Kitts, St. Vincent, Nevis, Trinidad, Tobago, St. Thomas, and Jamaica. Five thousand were converted and joined the Methodist churches.

William had to go via England to fulfill a promised engagement in Australia. The ship stopped in Ceylon, and he found a conference of ministers in session; thus, he providentially preached to them for five days on soul winning, and God used these five days to refire the ministers.

In 1869 William began a second fruitful fourteen months in campaigns in Australia and Tasmania, scattering holy fire. It was reported that God gave a "tidal wave of salvation"[5] in some places. Once more he stopped in Ceylon and spent three months of exhausting, God-honored labor.

IN INDIA

William was nearly fifty when he reached India on November 20, 1870. He evangelized Eurasians, Parsees, Hindus, and Muslims. He tried to found self-supporting churches wherever he went. The work in India grew greatly, and he became the superintendent of his self-supporting churches. He financed his ministry, travel, and family expenses without gifts from others, using funds from his books instead. He was always sacrificial for Jesus.

The work in India had been very difficult, particularly in unfruitful North India. William's first services in Allahabad and Lucknow were not especially fruitful, but within three weeks of arriving in Lucknow on November 25, 1870, God gave a mighty revival and more than one hundred were converted. A newer and higher standard of piety began to spread among the Christians. All that year the spirit of revival burned brightly among both Europeans and Indians. God worked so powerfully that some manifestations of the Spirit's salvation exceeded anything Bishop Thoburn, who had invited William to India, had seen in his lifetime.

Within three weeks in Kanpur, William organized two small churches. Then he went from one Methodist center to another as the conference leaders scheduled him. He preached in Kanpur, Shahjahanpur, Bareilly, Meerut, Delhi, and other cities. God used William's ministry to convict people of hidden sin. The tremendous power of his ministry resulted in repentance, confession, forgiveness of sins, and changed character. William went to Bombay in 1871. God gave revival through his vigorous evangelism, and a large number of fellowship bands were formed to carry on the work more deeply. The first of a large number was organized on December 30, 1871.

William began to receive more invitations to minister in other South Indian cities. Non-Christians were impressed by the morally changed lives of the converts; however, two daily papers and several preachers in Bombay opposed his methods and "sudden conversions." In spite of this opposition, William tried to make his evangelism a blessing and strength to all denominations. He advised converts to go back to their churches if they found spiritual help there, but soon his bands developed into a new group of churches.

The work did not cease with William's departure but kept on growing. He remained in the Bombay and Poona area for a full year. Then he began campaigning in Calcutta on January 12, 1873, with much the same outpouring of the Spirit in revival. A missionary observer said of William, "What a flame of revival he had become! The living God was with him and pentecostal fire fell upon the people wherever he went."[6]

IN SOUTH INDIA

On February 4, 1874, William sailed for Madras and began packing out a hall that seated three hundred people. He had thirty seekers the second night. Within one month he had formed eight fellowship bands. By June he had three centers within 207 miles. In Madras there were 335 members in eighteen churches in five months. William wanted the church in India to adapt to Indian customs and social structures and to be totally self-supporting. He did not want European-style buildings. The work he established became the South India Conference of the church, and he was superintendent of the whole conference.

As revival began to spread, William had to move to a larger hall seating six hundred, referring converts with Wesleyan or Baptist backgrounds to their own churches and organizing the other inquirers into new house churches. He then went to Bangalore and filled the available hall. In five weeks he had won 140 people to Christ, organized four fellowship bands, and planted another local church that became permanent, with more than a hundred converts. He also purchased two more church sites.

Commenting on the revivals in India, George Bowen, a renowned missionary to Bombay, said, "During the recent revivals under William Taylor's ministry preachers of established reputation have been found utterly useless in the work of leading souls to Christ."[7] Bishop J. M. Thoburn insisted that the revival influence of William's ministry was widely felt and marked the beginning of a new era in the mission field of India.

REVIVAL FIRE EVERYWHERE

Throughout William's life, evangelism, revival, and church planting were his priorities. He won souls to Christ and lit revival fires everywhere he went. In the early years on the mission field, he gladly cooperated with various Protestant groups and churches, much to the dismay of the Methodist hierarchy. It was at times very difficult for him to adjust to the structure and policies of Methodism, though he remained a Methodist to the end of his life.

William had now been separated from his wife and children for seven and a half years by their mutual agreement. For two and a half years he had diligently labored in America, selling books, preaching, and raising funds for India. For six and a half years more he headquartered in the United States. He spent about two years of that time on ministry in South America, and he made a trip in 1875 to London at the request of D. L. Moody to help in Moody's London and British campaigns.

The need of South America was impressed on his heart. Lacking funds, he traveled by steerage, but he called it the best voyage of his life. As much as time would allow, he surveyed the tremendous need, especially that of the unreached Indians. William's first trip to South America lasted six months and resulted in the opening of twelve centers for education and evangelism; within nine months workers were selected, appointed, and sent. He then began to establish self-supporting missions in South America. He requested that missionaries be financed by contributions from supporters (as faith missions do) and by tentmaking through tuition from teaching the local people. William even wrote a book called *Pauline Methods of Missionary Work*. Later he wrote another book called *Self-Supporting Missions*.

Was William so busy serving God that he had no time to deepen his own spiritual life? Listen to his testimony:

> I have been accustomed to walk with God for forty-four years without a break. Sometimes I have had a special manifestation to my spirit of the Son of God, when it was my pleasure to perceive his distinct personality, and sit in his presence and admire and adore him, and in melting love sympathize with him in his stupendous undertaking of bringing our lost race back to God, and feel the wish in my heart, "Oh, that I could multiply myself into a thousand, and give a thousand years to help Jesus."

At other times I have had a special manifestation of the personal Holy Ghost and the amazing "love of the Spirit" for a perishing world, and in adoring love, and sympathy put myself entirely at his disposal, to illuminate and lead me according to his own infinite wisdom and love.

But ever since I took charge of this expedition to Africa, with no less appreciation and admiration of the personal Jesus and the personal Holy Sanctifier, I have walked all these months in the manifestation of the personal presence of God the Father, with such enlarged perceptions of his wisdom, his love, his patience and forbearance, his infinite desire to adjust the human conditions essential to the fulfillment of his covenant-pledge to the Redeemer: "to give him the heathen for his inheritance, and the uttermost parts of the earth for his possession" [Ps. 2:8], I sit in his presence, and more than ever before weep in adoring love. His special providences over me and my charge have been continuous and most distinctly discernible.[8]

MISSIONARY BISHOP FOR AFRICA

In 1884, at age sixty-three, William was elected missionary bishop of Africa by the Methodist General Conference in the United States. He was not a candidate and was concerned that his election would interfere with his self-supporting missionary work. He was assured by various leaders that they wanted him to carry on as he had been doing. So he planted self-supporting missions in Angola, Liberia, Congo, and Mozambique.

After twelve years as missionary bishop, William was unexpectedly retired by the conference in May 1896. He accepted it like a soldier retired from active duty, saying, "I have for fifty-four years received my ministerial appointments from God."

William's wife came from California to join him at this last Methodist conference. They felt that rather than returning at once to California he should make the trip to South Africa he had been planning. He evangelized for eighteen months on this last visit and preached with power to large groups. In Queenstown six hundred Africans filled the church and one hundred knelt on the grass outside as they sought the Lord. William's uncompromising preaching gripped the hearts of many and brought them to the altar seeking peace, pardon, purity, and power.

Near the end of 1897 William felt that his Africa ministry was complete. His last week in a wild but heavily populated area he preached nine times in four days. Eighty tribal people were converted, and forty more were seeking as he left. In another village seventy-eight Africans fell on their knees before God and forty of them were saved. William's eighteen-month visit to Africa resulted in "the salvation of a large number of souls and the Christian people in the fields he visited were greatly edified."[9]

To Heaven

Only once in fifty-five years of ministry had William ever gone to bed because of illness (a case of the measles), but he almost died on his voyage to Liverpool before returning to the United States. He regained strength, sailed to New York, then journeyed by train to California. Returning home, he worked on a large book, *The Flaming Torch in Darkest Africa*. The world-renowned Henry M. Stanley, a friend of William's, wrote the introduction.

For five years William's health compelled him to rest. Nevertheless, he promised to pray for those on the fields, saying, "It would be my delight to join you in shouting for the battle for souls."[10] But his voice had failed. William was one who never turned back, never doubted, but was always ready to stand up for Jesus and trust God to supply all his needs. He was an outstanding example of the fruit of the Spirit we call self-control. He was incapacitated only five days before he died. God gave him several visions of heavenly scenes before he finally slept in Jesus on May 18, 1902, in Palo Alto, California, at the age of eighty-one.

Dr. J. Edwin Orr, historian of revival awakenings, writes, "The 1858 Awakening was extended to all six continents by the remarkable ministry of a very unusual Methodist, William Taylor, who proved to be one of the most versatile evangelists of all time, a follower of Wesley who made the world his parish in a way that few in history ever did."[11]

Epilogue

These have been brief accounts of fourteen men and women of God who served their Lord during the past five centuries. They are just a few of God's heroes. I chose these fourteen because all of them witnessed to an experience subsequent to their new birth when they were filled with God's Spirit. They may have used different terms to describe it, but all rejoiced in its blessed reality. I hope you too know the reality of such an infilling of God's Spirit in your life.

Will you join me in praying that more and more of God's children, regardless of their church background, will share this experience of a deeper holy life? I am now eighty-six, and this may be my last book. I pray for God's fullest blessing on your life, my beloved reader.

Notes

CHAPTER 1: FRANCIS ASBURY

1. Charles Ludwig, *Francis Asbury: God's Circuit Rider* (Milford, MI: Mott Media, 1984).
2. Ibid., 36.
3. Ibid., 54.
4. Ibid., 158.
5. Ibid., 158.
6. Ibid., 160–61.
7. Ibid., 86.
8. Ibid.
9. Ibid., 87.
10. Ibid., 94.
11. Ibid., 96.
12. Ibid., 78.
13. Ibid., 173.
14. Ibid., 175.
15. Ibid., 182.
16. Ibid., 183.
17. Maldwyn Edwards, *Francis Asbury* (Manchester, England: Penwork [Leeds] Ltd., 1972), 9.
18. Ludwig, *Francis Asbury*, 185.
19. Ibid., 189.

CHAPTER 2: DUNCAN CAMPBELL (PART 1)

1. Andrew Woolsey, *Duncan Campbell: A Biography* (Edinburgh: The Faith Mission, 1974), 121. Woolsey was Campbell's son-in-law.

2. Ibid., 122.
3. Ibid., 123.
4. Ibid., 132–33.
5. Ibid., 133.

Chapter 3: Duncan Campbell (Part 2)

1. Andrew Woolsey, *Duncan Campbell: A Biography* (Edinburgh: The Faith Mission, 1974), 157.
2. Ibid., 173.
3. Ibid., 180.
4. Ibid., 182.
5. Written at Faith Mission Bible College, Edinburgh, on October 20, 1958, after talking with Reverend Duncan Campbell.

Chapter 4: Oswald Chambers

1. Bertha Chambers, *Oswald Chambers: His Life and Work* (London: Simpkin Marshall, 1938). Except as noted, the citations in this chapter come from this biography.

According to David McCasland, author of a more recent biography of Chambers, the designation "Bertha Chambers" as the biographer is an error. Gertrude did not put her own name on the book as author or compiler; she did write a preface, which she signed with the initials "B.C."—Biddy Chambers. But she was mistakenly listed as Bertha Chambers (the name of one of Oswald's sisters) when the book was recorded in the British Library in London. That error has persisted in spite of various attempts to correct it. Bertha had nothing to do with the publication and distribution of his books. Interestingly, Oswald also had a sister named Gertrude, which is probably the reason that he chose a nickname for his wife. In contrast with Bertha, Gertrude did much to promote Oswald's works that were published by Biddy.

2. Ibid., 85.
3. Ibid., 82.
4. Ibid., 93.
5. Ibid., 95.
6. Ibid., 153.
7. Ibid., 104.
8. Ibid., 105.
9. Ibid., 117.
10. Ibid., 119.
11. Ibid., 137.
12. Ibid., 145.
13. Ibid., 155.

14. Ibid., 164.
15. Ibid., 158.
16. Ibid., 163.
17. Ibid., 170–71.
18. Ibid., 188.
19. Ibid., 201–2.
20. Ibid., 251.
21. Ibid., 282.
22. D. W. Lambert, *Oswald Chambers: An Unbribed Soul* (Burslem, Stoke-on-Trent, England: M.O.V.E. Press, 1975), 77.
23. Ibid., 79.
24. V. Raymond Edman, *They Found the Secret* (Grand Rapids: Zondervan, 1984), 37.
25. David McCasland, *Oswald Chambers: Abandoned to God* (Grand Rapids: Discovery House, 1993), 296.

CHAPTER 5: JONATHAN GOFORTH

1. Rosalind Goforth, *Goforth of China* (Grand Rapids: Zondervan, 1937), 80.
2. Kenneth Scott Latourette, *A History of Christian Missions in China* (Taipei: Cheng-Wen Publishing Co., 1970), 512.
3. Ibid., 516–17.
4. Goforth, *Goforth of China,* 135.
5. Ibid., 179.
6. Ibid., 204.
7. Ibid., 279.
8. Ibid., 349.

CHAPTER 6: MADAME GUYON (PART I)

1. Abbie C. Morrow, ed., *Sweet-smelling Myrrh* (Cincinnati: God's Revivalist Office, n.d.), 174.
2. Thomas C. Upham, *Life, Religious Opinions and Experience of Madame Guyon* (London: Allenson & Co., Ltd.), 94–95.
3. J. Gilchrist Lawson, *Deeper Experiences of Famous Christians* (Anderson, IN: Warner Press, 1911), 97.
4. Ibid., 98.
5. Morrow, *Sweet-smelling Myrrh,* 174.
6. Upham, *Life . . . of Madame Guyon,* 126.
7. Ibid., 130.
8. Lawson, *Deeper Experiences,* 103.
9. Ibid.

CHAPTER 7: MADAME GUYON (PART 2)

1. Abbie C. Morrow, ed., *Sweet-smelling Myrrh* (Cincinnati: God's Revivalist Office, n.d.), 174.
2. Ibid., 48.
3. Ibid., 189.
4. Ibid., 190.
5. Ibid., 156–57.
6. Ibid., 158–59.
7. Ibid., 109.
8. Ibid., 116.
9. Ibid., 151.
10. Ibid., 155.
11. Ibid., 192.

CHAPTER 8: FRANCES RIDLEY HAVERGAL

1. J. Gilchrist Lawson, *Deeper Experiences of Famous Christians* (Anderson, IN: Warner Press, 1911), 314.
2. Ibid., 315.
3. Ibid., 317.
4. Ibid., 318–19.
5. Ibid., 319.
6. Ibid., 319–20.
7. Ibid., 320.
8. Ibid., 321.
9. Ibid.
10. Ibid., 321–22.
11. Ibid., 323.
12. Clara McLeister, *Men and Women of Deep Piety* (Cincinnati: God's Bible School and Revivalist, 1920), 234.
13. Lawson, *Deeper Experiences of Famous Christians*, 325.
14. McLeister, *Men and Women of Deep Piety*, 236.

CHAPTER 9: JOHN HYDE

1. Basil Miller, *Praying Hyde: A Man of Prayer* (Grand Rapids: Zondervan, 1943), 17.
2. Ibid., 19.
3. Ibid.
4. Ibid., 20.
5. Ibid., 23.
6. Ibid., 37.
7. Ibid., 42.
8. Ibid.

9. Ibid., 43.

10. Ibid., 78.

11. Ibid., 88, 93.

12. Ibid., 102.

13. Ibid., 125.

14. Ibid., 126.

15. Ibid., 83–84.

CHAPTER 11: ADONIRAM JUDSON (PART 2)

1. Courtney Anderson, *To the Golden Shore* (Boston: Little, Brown and Co., 1956; reprint, Grand Rapids: Zondervan, 1972), 495.

2. Ibid., 496.

3. Ibid., 499.

4. Ibid., 501.

CHAPTER 12: DWIGHT LYMAN MOODY

1. J. Gilchrist Lawson, *Deeper Experiences of Famous Christians* (Anderson, IN: Warner Press, 1911), 345.

2. R. A. Torrey, *Why God Used D. L. Moody* (Chicago: Moody Press, 1923), 55.

3. Lawson, *Deeper Experiences of Famous Christians,* 348.

4. Ibid.

5. Torrey, *Why God Used D. L. Moody,* 57–58.

6. Richard Elsworth Day, *Bush Aglow* (Grand Rapids: Baker, 1936), 311.

7. Ibid., 315–16.

8. Ibid., 317.

9. Ibid., 320.

10. Ibid., 329.

11. V. Raymond Edman, *They Found the Secret* (Grand Rapids: Zondervan, 1984), 76–77.

12. Torrey, *Why God Used D. L. Moody,* 52.

CHAPTER 13: EVAN ROBERTS

1. Eifion Evans, *The Welsh Revival of 1904* (Bryntirion, Wales: Evangelical Movement of Wales/Bryntirion Press, 1969), 141.

2. Wesley L. Duewel, *Revival Fire* (Grand Rapids: Zondervan, 1995), 185.

3. Evans, *Welsh Revival,* 70.

4. Ibid., 79.

5. D. M. Phillips, *Evan Roberts: The Great Welsh Revivalist and His Work* (London: Marshall Brothers, 1923), 161.

6. Ibid., 171.

7. Duewel, *Revival Fire,* 14. Written in Moriah Chapel, Loughor, Gorseinon, South Wales, September 24, 1964. The Welsh sing this poem to the tune *Stella* in their hymnal.

8. David Matthews, *I Saw the Welsh Revival* (Chicago: Moody Bible Institute, 1951), 38.

9. Ibid., 171.

10. Ibid., 172–73.

11. Ibid., 180.

12. Written in Penrheol, Gorseinon, Glams, South Wales, after service in Gospel Hall, September 23, 1964. Tune: *Stella.*

CHAPTER 14: GIROLAMO SAVONAROLA

1. J. Gilchrist Lawson, *Deeper Experiences of Famous Christians* (Anderson, IN: Warner Press, 1911), 73.

CHAPTER 15: AMANDA SMITH

1. Amanda Smith, *Autobiography of Amanda Smith: "Amanda Smith's Own Story."* (Chicago: Meyer & Brother, Publishers, 1893), 62.

2. Ibid., 79; quoted by D. W. Lambert, *Heralds of Holiness* (Burslem, Stoke-on-Trent, England: M.O.V.E. Press, 1975), 53.

3. Smith, *Autobiography of Amanda Smith,* 79.

4. Ibid., 284.

5. Ibid., 448.

6. Ibid., 487.

7. Publication clipping; source unknown.

CHAPTER 16: JOHN SMITH (PART 1)

1. George B. Kulp, *The Calloused Knees* (Cincinnati: God's Revivalist Office, 1909), 42.

2. Ibid., 68–69.

3. Ibid., 49.

4. Ibid., 50.

5. Ibid., 60–61.

6. Ibid., 62.

7. Ibid., 81.

8. Ibid., 83.

9. Ibid., 76.

10. Ibid., 77–78.

11. Ibid., 89–90.

12. Ibid., 89.

13. Ibid., 102–3.

14. Ibid., 103–4.
15. Ibid., 193–94.
16. Ibid., 202.
17. Ibid., 203–4.
18. Ibid., 201–5.

CHAPTER 17: JOHN SMITH (PART 2)

1. George B. Kulp, *The Calloused Knees* (Cincinnati: God's Revivalist Office, 1909), 118.
2. Ibid., 137–38.
3. Ibid., 139.
4. Ibid., 160.
5. Ibid., 157.
6. Ibid., 168–69.
7. Ibid., 171.
8. Ibid., 178.
9. Ibid., 281.
10. Ibid., 282.

CHAPTER 18: WILLIAM TAYLOR

1. Robert E. Speer, *Servants of the King* (New York: Young People's Missionary Movement of the United States and Canada, 1909), 38.
2. Ibid.
3. Ibid., 53.
4. Ibid., 143.
5. Ibid., 171.
6. John N. Hollister, *The Centenary of the Methodist Church in Southern Asia* (Lucknow, India: Lucknow Publishing House of the Methodist Church in Southern Asia, 1956), 123.
7. J. Edwin Orr, *Evangelical Awakenings in India* (New Delhi, India: Masihi Sahitya Sanstha, 1970), 49.
8. Publication clipping, source unknown.
9. John Paul, *The Soul Digger, or Life and Times of William Taylor* (Upland, IN: Taylor University Press, 1928), 287.
10. David Bundy, "Bishop William Taylor and Methodist Mission: A Study in Nineteenth-Century Social History, Part 2," Methodist History 28 (October 1989):199.
11. J. Edwin Orr, *Evangelical Awakenings in India* (New Delhi, India: Masihi Sahitya Sanstha, 1970), 49.

Bibliography

Anderson, Courtney. *To the Golden Shore*. Boston: Little, Brown, 1956; reprint, Grand Rapids: Zondervan, 1972.

Bly, Tacey, editor. *The Poems and Hymns of Christ's Sweet Singer, Frances Ridley Havergal*. New Canaan, CT: Keats, 1977.

Bone, Gratia Hyde, and Mary Hyde Hall, editors. *Life and Letters of Praying Hyde*. Springfield, IL: Williamson Press, n.d.

Bundy, David. "Bishop William Taylor and Methodist Mission: A Study in Nineteenth-Century Social History (Part 1)." *Methodist History* 27 (July 1989): 147–210.

———— . "Bishop William Taylor and Methodist Mission: A Study in Nineteenth-Century Social History (Part 2)." *Methodist History* 28 (October 1989): 3–21.

Carré, E. G. *Praying Hyde: A Challenge to Prayer*. 3d ed. London: Pickering & Inglis, n.d.

Chambers, Bertha. *Oswald Chambers: His Life and Work*. London: Simpkin Marshall Ltd., 1938.

Day, Richard Ellsworth. *Bush Aglow*. Grand Rapids: Baker, 1936.

Duewel, Wesley L. *Revival Fire*. Grand Rapids: Zondervan, 1995.

Edman, V. Raymond. *They Found the Secret*. Grand Rapids: Zondervan, 1984.

Edwards, Maldwyn. *Francis Asbury*. Manchester, England: Penwork (Leeds) Ltd., 1972.

Evans, Eifion. *The Welsh Revival of 1904*. Bryntirion, Wales: Evangelical Movement of Wales/Bryntirion Press, 1969.

Goforth, Rosalind. *Goforth of China.* Grand Rapids: Zondervan, 1937.

Hollister, John N. *The Centenary of the Methodist Church in Southern Asia.* Lucknow, India: Lucknow Publishing House of the Methodist Church in Southern Asia, 1956.

Judson, Edward. *The Life of Adoniram Judson.* New York: Anson D. F. Randolph & Co., 1883.

Kulp, George B. *The Calloused Knees.* Cincinnati: God's Revivalist Office, 1909.

Lambert, D. W. *Heralds of Holiness.* Burslem, Stoke-on-Trent, England: M.O.V.E. Press, 1975.

_____ . *Oswald Chambers: An Unbribed Soul.* Fort Washington, PA: Christian Literature Crusade, 1983.

Latourette, Kenneth Scott. *A History of Christian Missions in China.* Taipei: Cheng-Wen Publishing Co., 1970.

Lawson, J. Gilchrist. *Deeper Experiences of Famous Christians.* Anderson, IN: Warner Press, 1911.

Ludwig, Charles. *Francis Asbury: God's Circuit Rider.* Milford, MI: Mott Media, 1984.

McCasland, David. *Oswald Chambers: Abandoned to God.* Grand Rapids: Discovery House, 1993.

McLeister, Clara. *Men and Women of Deep Piety.* Cincinnati: God's Bible School and Revivalist, 1920.

Matthews, David. *I Saw the Welsh Revival.* Chicago: Moody Bible Institute, 1951.

Miller, Basil. *Praying Hyde: A Man of Prayer.* Grand Rapids: Zondervan, 1943.

Morrow, Abbie C., ed. *Sweet-smelling Myrrh.* Cincinnati: God's Revivalist Office, n.d. (introduction written June 6, 1898).

Orr, J. Edwin. *Evangelical Awakenings in India.* New Delhi: Masihi Sahitya Sanstha, 1970.

Paul, John. *The Soul Digger, or Life and Times of William Taylor.* Upland, IN: Taylor University Press, 1928.

Phillips, D. M. *Evan Roberts: The Great Welsh Revivalist and His Work.* London: Marshall Brothers, 1923.

Smith, Amanda. *Autobiography of Amanda Smith: "Amanda Smith's Own Story."* Chicago: Meyer & Brother, Publishers, 1893.

Speer, Robert E. *Servants of the King.* New York: Young People's Missionary Movement of the United States and Canada, 1909.

Taylor, William. *Street Preaching in San Francisco.* Edited by W. P. Strickland. New York: Carlton & Porter, 1856.

————— . *Ten Years of Self-Supporting Missions in India.* New York: Phillips & Hunt, 1882.

Torrey, R. A. *Why God Used D. L. Moody.* Chicago: Moody Press, 1923.

Upham, Thomas C. *Life, Religious Opinions and Experience of Madame Guyon.* London: Allenson & Co., 1947.

Verphoegh, Harry, editor. *Oswald Chambers: The Best from All His Books.* Nashville: Oliver Nelson, 1987.

Woolsey, Andrew. *Duncan Campbell: A Biography.* Edinburgh: The Faith Mission, 1974.

GOD HAS A MORE EFFECTIVE PRAYER LIFE FOR YOU THAN YOU EVER DREAMED POSSIBLE.

Mighty Prevailing Prayer
Wesley L. Duewel

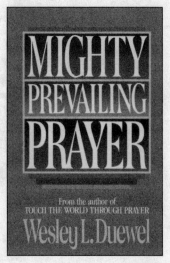

Let this volume be your open door to wonderful answers to prayer. Here is your personal guide to a life of mighty prevailing prayer. Let this book speak to your heart, take you to your knees, and help you obtain prayer answers in difficult and resistant situations.

Leonard Ravenhill calls it an "encyclopedia" you will want to read and refer to it again and again. It is a lifetime investment, a marvelous balance, and a mandate for and a means of prevailing prayer. The evangelical church is guilty of the sin of prayerlessness. Wesley Duewel has provided exactly what we need: a biblically sound exposition of prevailing prayer and practical suggestions for ways to prevail in prayer.

Softcover: 0-310-36191-5

PICK UP A COPY AT YOUR FAVORITE BOOKSTORE!

ZONDERVAN™

GRAND RAPIDS, MICHIGAN 49530 USA

WWW.ZONDERVAN.COM

Revival Fire
Wesley L. Duewel

Fire blazes from heaven, and a stone altar erupts in flame. So begins a spiritual awakening, the kindling of a revival fire still burning today. Beginning with Elijah and God's tremendous one-day revival of Israel, Wesley Duewel tells stories of revivals spanning the globe from America to China to Africa, all brought about by obedience and heartfelt prayer. He illustrates how God has used revival fire through the centuries to revive the church and reveal the glorious presence of the Holy Spirit.

Softcover: 0-310-49661-6

PICK UP A COPY AT YOUR FAVORITE BOOKSTORE!

GRAND RAPIDS, MICHIGAN 49530 USA

WWW.ZONDERVAN.COM

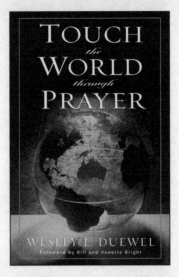

Touch the World through Prayer

Wesley L. Duewel

"God has a wonderful plan by which you can have a world influence through your prayer," writes Dr. Wesley Duewel. "God has planned that ordinary Christians like you and me can become mighty in prayer for the reaping of Christ's harvest among the nations today."

Touch the World through Prayer explains how every Christian can pray for the missionaries, church leaders, and political leaders in countries around the globe where the gospel is being preached today. Dr. Duewel gives specific Bible promises that we can claim in these intercessory prayers.

He describes how to pray in the power of Jesus' name, how to counteract the influence of Satan, how to recognize the work of angels in answer to prayer, and much more. *Touch the World through Prayer* provides step-by-step plans for making a prayer list, organizing a prayer circle, and holding a prayer retreat for your Christian friends who have a burden for missions.

Softcover: 0-310-36271-7

We want to hear from you. Please send your comments about this book to us in care of the address below. Thank you.

ZONDERVAN™

GRAND RAPIDS, MICHIGAN 49530 USA

WWW.ZONDERVAN.COM